LEADERSICK

Becoming a Healthy Leader

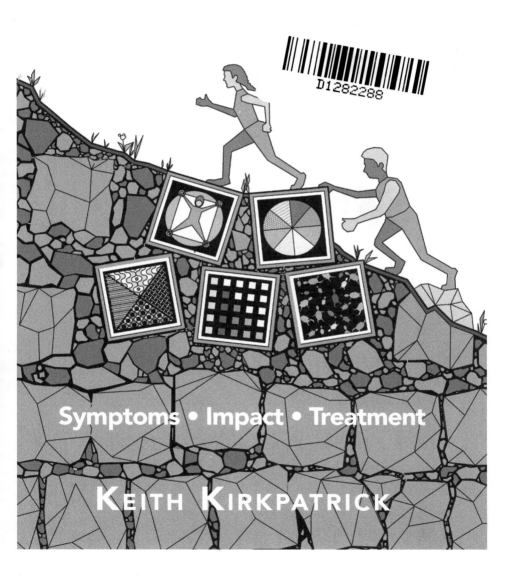

Symptoms • Impact • Treatment

KEITH KIRKPATRICK

LEADERSICK
Becoming a Healthy Leader
Copyright © 2022 by Keith Kirkpatrick

First Edition
ISBN 979-8-218-08178-2

KPM Group, Inc. Valparaiso, Indiana
LeadersickBook.com

DEDICATION

To *George Miga* who told me I had the talent to write. I hope he was right.

To *Chip Lesch* who encouraged me to write and told me it would be worth it. It seems he might be right.

To my dad, **Bob Kirkpatrick**, who gave me a reason to write: to help others in any way I could. And he was right.

Lastly, to the college English professor, a name I cannot remember, who told me I had no ability to write . . . I'm not sure I deserved a D.

"I've experienced several different healing methodologies over the years – counseling, self-help seminars, and I've read a lot – but none of them will work unless you really want to heal."
Lindsay Wagner, actress, model, author

"The place of true healing is a fierce place. It's a giant place. It's a place of monstrous beauty and endless dark and glimmering light. And you have to work really, really, really hard to get there, but you can do it."
Cheryl Strayed, bestselling author, podcast host

"Healing may not be so much about getting better, as about letting go of everything that isn't you – all of the expectations, all of the beliefs – and becoming who you are."
Rachel Naomi Remen, physician, author, teacher

"Healing is embracing what is most feared; healing is opening what has been closed, softening what has hardened into obstruction, healing is learning to trust life."
Jeanne Achterberg, psychologist, pioneer

Contents

Self   Assignment

Style   Capacity   People

LEADERSICK DISEASES

Index of Diseases

SELF – Group A

What you understand about yourself.
Self-perception, self-awareness.

CAPACITY – Group B

What your load is.
Balance, boundaries, limitations.

STYLE – Group C

How you handle your role.
Methods, philosophy, framework.

ASSIGNMENT – Group D
Who does the work.
Allocation, designation, responsibility.

PEOPLE – Group E

How you treat those you lead.
Interactions, relationships.

INTRODUCTION

Being a leader is a tough job, and no one knows that better than a leader. There are extreme highs and some very serious lows. There are times we perform incredibly well, and at other times, not so great. When our leadership suffers, we feel as if we are sick. It's like having an illness, a malady, a condition.

I have been a leader practically my whole life and an educator in the fields of leadership and entrepreneurship for nearly 30 years. As a practitioner, I know what it is like to be in the leadership trenches. To prove it, I have my share of scars and ample quantity of awards.

As an educator I have listened to stories and experiences of others as they shared amazing outcomes, exhilarating feelings, inspirational moments, and enlightened discoveries. I have also heard about the failures, fractures, disappointments, missed goals, and hard-hitting lessons.

As I considered these pitfalls, mistakes, errors, and problems which befall leaders, it seemed there was an abundance of commonality with the medical concepts of disease diagnosis, impact, and treatment. By analyzing, organizing, and categorizing these leadership challenges, I was able to name and define an extensive list of ailments which I call **leadership diseases.**

This book is not like any other book on leadership. Knowing that leaders sometimes take themselves too seriously, I ventured a different approach for looking at yourself and trying to figure out what's wrong. Similar to how we handle diseases, we often won't talk about what is happening to us, and we sometimes just ignore it. Having one or more of these diseases means you are Leadersick.

Leadersick – Becoming a Healthy Leader is meant to enlighten you, challenge your thinking, and provide you with choices. It is not definitively prescriptive, nor does it provide a proven formula, give you all the answers, or describe the right way.

Experiencing a disease can force you to rest, rebuild, and make you stronger. It can also *kick your butt*. No one really wants to be sick; we want to be healthy. And we all know – **when leaders get better, we all get better.**

Leadersick Defined

There are a variety of terms which are used to describe when someone is in this broad classification of being sick or having an illness. Throughout the book, we interchange a number of terms similar to the word *disease* such as: ailment, malady, illness, disorder, disability, condition, disease, affliction, attack, and infection, or ill, unwell, infected, disabled, and incapacitated.

Many of these terms are interchangeable or will have a better fit as you read the book. In each word used there may be minor differences or slight nuances in the definitions. Some terms may require you to infer various levels of severity or types of sickness. Each word is filtered or modified by our perceptions, understanding, knowledge, and experience. As you read, use the term which best fits, is more familiar, or is more comfortable for you.

Try to avoid arguing or challenging the words selected within the book. Substitute or convert them into what works for you. All of these terms or choices have been combined into one term for all leadership diseases, and it is **leadersick**.

Why We Call Them Diseases

If you live on this planet, you will experience disease in your life, whether physical or mental. No one is immune. Similarly, if you are in leadership roles, you are going to have times when you feel lousy, you have no energy, or you can't function at your normal levels. Something takes you down or puts you out. You experience periods in your leadership life when your effectiveness is reduced, significantly impaired, or fully damaged.

Looking at a couple of definitions for the word disease, you can see the parallel with what ails you as a leader. One definition describes "a disorder of structure or function in a human, animal, or plant, especially one that has known cause and a distinctive group of symptoms, signs, or anatomical changes" (lexico.com). Another says "a particular quality, habit, or disposition regarded as adversely affecting a person or group of people" (lexico.com). Whether we call it a malady, disorder, or ailment, you are sick, and **disease** seemed to be the right word choice.

For some, the word disease stirs very negative feelings and generates thoughts of pain, suffering, and perhaps death. The COVID global pandemic created a heightened awareness for some of what a disease can do on a large scale, and others view it as not so important or something not to be feared. No matter your perspective, disease is something that touches all of us, even if in different ways or by other words as mentioned above.

Who Is a Leader?

I have a broad definition of leadership and believe nearly everyone has the potential to lead. During presentations I have made over the years, I frequently asked, "Are you a leader?" Some raised their hands, others did not. My follow up questions were the following: "How many of you are parents? How many are teachers or have coached? Have you led activities for kids or adults?" As these queries were made, more hands were raised, and that's when I tell them, "If you raised your hand at any time, you are a leader," whether or not you realize it, or whether or not you are good at it.

The concepts in this book can and will apply to many roles in leadership whether your efforts are as an employee or a volunteer. Leadership includes a broad range of roles and time investments. It requires various levels of commitment and talent utilization. Some leadership issues seem very specific to work situations, but many are related to non-employment situations.

Wisdom of Real Leaders

My involvement in leadership development has given me the opportunity to teach, coach, and mentor hundreds of leaders. I have created and managed programs, classes, and training for leaders. I have had the privilege throughout my career to work with a wide variety of leaders from all types of backgrounds, careers, arenas of service, sectors, demographics, and experiences.

This book is filled with the wisdom of everyday leaders who operate at the ground level. These are leaders who are business owners, CEOs, police chiefs, superintendents, university administrators, government officials, bank officers, and executive directors. They are also teachers, supervisors, coaches, team leaders, project coordinators, program planners, and organizers. Their names and backgrounds are presented at the end of the book.

From these ranks of several thousand leaders, I selected, surveyed, and interviewed a group of nearly 100 who represented solid examples of good, if not great, leadership. I have presented my methodology along with the names of those who helped on this book toward the end as well.

All of these people are not only leaders in their places of employment, but also in their communities and families. They are board members, club presidents, chairpersons, as well as service and activity volunteers. They may not be big names or famous people, but they lead every day. Their real-life experiences contributed to the content of this book.

How Diseases Were Chosen

As I put this book together, I focused on the frailties and pitfalls people experienced in their leadership roles. Excluded were what might be classified as common character flaws, bad habits, and weaknesses of people in their everyday lives. Can a leader be obnoxious, a poor time manager, or easy to anger? Of course, but so can just about everyone else. Being rude and crude are just bad personal traits. These more common personal problems were avoided and not selected as leadership diseases.

My focus for the diseases were certain aspects of leadership which have a specific kind of negative impact on the person in that role. Similar to physical and mental illness, when these ailments appear, they can affect a leader's ability to function. As I identified these ailments, they were assigned fitting names that help identify what the diseases are and the damage they inflict.

My Story

It seemed a good idea to begin this book with some personal reflection on my leadership roles and my own leadership health. The motto of "Doctor, heal thyself" could be shifted to "Doctor, diagnose thyself." Well, I am not a doctor. But if I am asking my readers to apply this book to their leadership lives, I should be willing to use it and understand how sick I was at one time in my leadership life.

Toward the end of a 12-year tenure as CEO of an organization, I began to get restless. I knew I did not want to remain in this role forever, and at some point, I would or should move on. After unsuccessfully attempting to find someone to groom as my successor, the board and I developed a succession plan which ultimately did not yield the results we were hoping. It was tough as I continued to wrestle with the decision and finally announced my departure.

As the board moved forward with transition to new leadership, I remained in a limited role with the organization through two Interim CEOs and eventually a new leader. During that time, major decisions were made to dramatically change the organization's direction and programming.

As I look back, my discomfort, stress, sleeplessness, and pain should have been signs or signals that something was wrong with me. I struggled through it but at personal cost. After my complete exit from the organization, the idea for this book began to take shape. Since the concept of leadership diseases was not around then, I could not analyze my experience, but now I can by using this book as a tool.

My diagnosis begins with two diseases I have battled my whole life: EXPLATONOMY defined as too much on your plate, and EXOCARDIO, being overly passionate for your cause. By reviewing my symptoms and understanding the impact they were having on me, I could have reached a better understanding and embarked upon my recovery much earlier and much quicker.

If I had recognized my case of EXPLATONOMY, perhaps I could have realized the need to make changes or get recharged. Instead, my load began to slowly wear me out.

The second affliction, EXOCARDIO, was generated by my acting as an unbounded champion while expanding our programs. My passion and commitment drove me to work excessive hours as I invested myself deeper and deeper into our cause. Instead, I could have considered slowing down and stabilizing what we already had.

The next two diseases were lesser cases but mostly induced by my actions. DYNAMOPEXY was when I relied on my reputation to carry me. Surely everyone could see the sacrifices I had made and appreciate the incredible outcomes we were generating. When they did not, I was infected. Additionally, I think I had a touch of EGOMEGALY. It affected me because I thought I was right, and the way we did it was the way it should be done. That is a pretty consistent symptom of that disorder.

The four previous diseases had weakened me and then COMPASSLESS hit. I was not handling the changes very well. I think the first four had taken their toll. I had expectations of what my life would be like after I stepped down and let go, but none of those were coming to fruition. I also took on a bit of BCT (BLAMCRITONOMY) where I was blaming and criticizing others for how they were handling things.

As this set of maladies began to dissipate or come under control, two new ones struck. The first was NOMADIA. I felt lost, trying to find my next path forward. It was tough to watch the changes being made without having much input or control. Then, OPTOPENIA appeared. OPTOPENIA is about having a lack of vision and getting no buy in from others. Actually, I had developed this disease long before, but I did not recognize it.

Evidently, I had not conveyed the vision and expectations clearly enough for others to fully understand the big picture, appreciate the foundation which had been laid, value the impact, realize the potential, and commit to growth. My OPTOPENIA was evidenced by my inability or failure to educate and sell the board on this vision. Even if I knew about the affliction and had recognized it, the damage was already done.

Any good story should end with the final outcomes of recovery and healing. I could have taken more time to explain how my diagnosis occurred and provided more detail on how the impact of the ailment affected me and the organization.

I consider my treatment to have been successful and the larger portion of my recovery is in the past. The healing continues though. Needless to say, the writing of this book has been part of my therapy. I hope it is found useful for other leaders to help them understand and address their leadership diseases.

PURPOSE

Because you are looking at this book, its title or potential content must have intrigued you. You probably wondered if you have a leadership disease or maybe more than one. During their journeys, all leaders will experience some form of one or more of the diseases presented in this book. No one is exempt from at least one or more of these sicknesses or at one level or another.

You might be thinking one or more of the following: "Which do I have? What have I had? I wonder what others think they have. I can't wait to diagnose my boss, the board chair, or a close friend. How about those I think are bad leaders? They must be completely infected. How is this book going to explain each disease and make it relevant to me?" These are great questions, which this book will seek to address.

Leadersick – Becoming a Healthy Leader is not designed to give you **all** the answers or provide the reader with an exact diagnosis and a specific remedy tailored to a person's individual condition. It cannot fully prevent you from ever having a leadership disease. Rather, it will offer suggestions and alternatives to help you.

The book's intention is to sensitize you to the fact that:

- You and your leadership are not perfect – everyone has at least some deficits.

- There are a number of different ways for leaders to be ineffective – leadership is a complex mix of art and science.

- Your leadership has an effect on those around you – those who you serve and those who serve you are impacted by how effective (healthy) or ineffective (sick) you are as a leader.

- All hope is not lost – there are some remedies embedded here that will at least help you improve what you and your organization accomplish.

It will likely cause you to look more closely at yourself, challenge assumptions you make about people and processes, and even help you understand how and why people see things differently. It will help you understand yourself by learning how each disease impacts you and those you lead. It will help you analyze and compare other leaders. It may cause you to look more closely at yourself, challenge assumptions you make, and understand how and why people see things differently.

There is an abundance of great books on leadership. *Leadersick – Becoming a Healthy Leader* is a different approach, designed to make you think in a new way. Rather than focus on just the successful strategies many great leaders have employed, it takes a step or two back to figure out why new approaches are necessary in today's world. You may even find yourself motivated to research, read, or rediscover other topics on leadership which specifically relate to helping you with your ailments.

Application

Leaders often take themselves too seriously. They don't necessarily like to look at their leadership mistakes, problems, and pitfalls. *Leadersick* offers an avenue for thinking about these issues in a lighter way. It can create conversations on a *not so often* talked about subject. In can create a common language and format for analysis.

Read it by yourself and allow it to help you evaluate your leadership. Buy it for someone so you can talk about the diseases and make comparisons. It could be a discussion guide with a specific group of people such as a class, professional association, study group, board of directors, or work team.

Use it with your friends or family. Share it within an organization or workplace. Let it help guide your conversations with those you lead or with those who lead you. A mentor, guide, or coach might wish to use it to help a leader understand some particular aspect of leadership.

Reviewing the diseases in this book may be a difficult task. You may take it personally, feel it hit you hard, even really upset you. That means the book is doing its job to make you aware. Take it seriously, but do not let it derail you. Consider your emotional arousal as an opportunity to learn something about yourself, face your challenges, and become healthier as a leader.

Your Reading Style

Some of you will pick up this book and read it from beginning to end. Others will skip around. Some will just jump into the diseases immediately looking for the ones you think you might have or determining the ones with which your co-workers, friends, bosses, and prominent leaders are afflicted.

If you are a person who reads a book from front to back, you may find yourself overwhelmed as you read about each disease in sequence. You may question what you think is missing, why descriptions and explanations are limited, where is the part about _____? If this happens, you may want to turn to the last chapters and read them. There you will find information which may help you gain a greater understanding and put things into a better perspective. Maybe some of your burning concerns will be addressed.

If you are a scanner or have great fun just flipping around, you should take some time to read the front portion of the book to help you understand why this book was written, how it is constructed, and how to best use it. There are some significant reasons for why major issues appear to be missing from the disease descriptions.

If you are a searcher attempting to diagnose yourself immediately or determine what is wrong with those around you, stop and spend time looking at the front and back ends of the book. It may put things in perspective and help you gain more from its content.

Perspectives

If you are reading this book, the assumption is that you are a leader or are interested in leadership. It is written to directly apply to **you**, asking questions about how you feel and what you are experiencing. You will be referred to as a **leader**.

The term **people** is continually used to refer to your employees, team, board members, class, volunteers, committee members, project group, or any other collection of folks who look to you as a leader or as their leader. Some might label these people as followers. I prefer not to use that term because good leaders find themselves in those roles from time to time. Good leaders know when to follow and often view their people as a group of leaders or at least potential leaders.

When we talk about **organizations**, we are referring to all types of entities, whether business, government, or non-profit, as well as clubs, boards, associations, and religions. Organizations often have a formal or legal structure. We also use the term **teams,** meaning committees, classes, athletics, projects, or work units; any type of group where people are assembled to accomplish something. Organizations and teams are used interchangeably.

Nature of Disease

Leadership diseases have much commonality with the wide range of illnesses we experience with our bodies and our minds. The comparisons lead me to believe that the problems presented in this book are, indeed, diseases.

First, everyone knows it is nearly impossible to go through life without getting sick or hurt. Can you think of anyone who has not had a single health issue in life? Leaders experience the same situation. You cannot go through your leadership life without contracting a leadership disease from time to time.

A leadership disease may be chronic because you just cannot seem to shake it. You may have a genetic pre-disposition, if you are generally grumpy, perpetually pessimistic, or fearful of conflict, to name a few. You may be highly susceptible to certain diseases because your personality plays into it easily, you were never exposed to it, or your cultural or life experiences leave you short of the skills or knowledge to handle it.

An event can even hit you directly with sudden impact or through unexpected events. You did not even see it coming. You were *voluntold* to lead. The current leader or leaders suddenly disappear, and you are next in line. You step into the middle of a situation, and everyone turns to you for leadership. Accidents also happen to leaders. Suddenly, you have a leadership disease.

We also know that most common ailments impact you in a holistic way. If you are hurt physically, it affects your brain, emotions, and spirit. You can mix these in many ways to always find everything is impacted. It is the same with a leadership disease, whichever one it may be; your mind, body, heart, and soul are changed in negative ways. It is not just a mental health issue.

Learning and prevention are extremely helpful. They may help you avoid certain afflictions more readily, yet they may help reduce the frequency of contraction, lessen the impact, or quicken recovery. When you experience some leadership diseases, you may build immunity, sometimes with a single contraction. There are even ways to be inoculated without a needle. Taking precaution prior to exposure, having a mentor guide you, being forewarned, or watching someone else go through it could be a leader's way of avoiding a specific disease.

Because of these close parallels of health, well-being, and medical care depicted above, I have analyzed, named, defined, and explained leadership diseases in a way similar to the health concerns that are already familiar in our lives.

You will note that there is little or no reference to ethnicity or demographics because leadership diseases hit everyone. Yet, we realize that these descriptions and conditions may be influenced by the very important nuances that make us different, our education level, what we look like, where we are from, our cultural upbringing, and any other characteristics which classify people. Age may be the one factor where there is more noticeable impact, but it's more about experience level than years on the planet.

Although no one is fully immune, some leaders may be more susceptible to certain kinds of diseases than others. The intention of this book is to introduce a wide variety of leadership diseases for reflection and examination. Those differences may be worthy of discovery and analysis at some point in the future. Until then, we invite you to move into your own personal discovery of how you are impacted by your own uniqueness.

Disease Presentation Format

This book is structured similarly to that found in medical journals and health reference books. In those publications, professionals analyze, define, and diagnose diseases. The 28 diseases are located in the center of the book. Each leadership disease has its own chapter which is organized using the same format.

The diseases are arranged into five groups or perspectives organized by disease similarities. This division will provide the reader with a simpler way to grasp the contents in each category facilitating a better understanding of the diseases:

1. Self - What you understand about yourself.
2. Capacity - What your load is.
3. Style - How you address your role.
4. Assignment - Who does the work.
5. People - How you treat those you lead.

CLASSIFICATION

Each chapter begins with the **Disease Name** and is followed by its **Pronunciation**, how it might be said. A short **Description** provides a brief definition of the disease. The **Derivation** is an explanation of how the name for the disease was formulated.

SYMPTOMS - Signs & Causes

Each disease begins with a **list of conditions** that may signal your having contracted it. It's the **WHAT is going on** or **WHY it is occurring.** It might be what you are doing, what is happening around you, and what you are experiencing. In some ways it's like a checklist, which means if you can say Yes to it or can rate the intensity, it will help you determine whether you have it or not. These factors are derived from how you feel or what you believe. They may be what you are telling yourself and sometimes verbally expressing in a whisper or to others. Other signs may come from how others see you or what others are doing in response to you.

IMPACT - Risk Factors, Stages & Outcomes

Depending on the quantity, frequency, and intensity of the symptoms, this section will offer **examples of what is happening or may happen if you have the disease.** It does not mean that all of these will occur or even speculate on the magnitude of any of them. They will help you gauge what you may be risking, how the disease progresses, or what may be the final or long-lasting impact of the disease upon you, those who follow you, and the organization affiliated with your leadership efforts.

TREATMENT - Remedy, Prevention & Control

As with all diseases, you have **options to facilitate your healing or assist you in addressing the disease.** They may help you reduce or delay the impact, possibly even avoid or prevent a future occurrence. There are all kinds of suggestions or ideas presented in this section. The question is which will work for you. You may want to research the recommendations. There are many books already written to expand on almost all the ideas presented. Of course, these treatments are often more effective when you are assisted or supported by a person or team of people who know how to guide, direct, or instruct you.

Diagnosis = Symptoms + Impact

For the most part, this book is written as a self-diagnostic tool. Each chapter is meant to make you **think and reflect on yourself.** You should know yourself better than anyone else does. Most likely you understand the strength of your resolve to make a personal commitment to diagnosis and treatment. You will determine what applies to you. You may ask: Can people really diagnose themselves? Do they know the symptoms, causes, and signs? I will ask you: Can you tell when you are sick? Do you know when something does not feel or seem right?

The first step with any disease is to recognize it. It begins with a review and evaluation of the symptoms. Which ones have I experienced? What's going on within and around me? What am I noticing or overlooking? What are people telling me? How many of these symptoms are applicable to me and at what level of intensity?

It is for you, often with the help of another, to assess these factors and determine a diagnosis or finding. You may conclude with one of the following:

- I am in the early stages of contracting it.
- Yes, I have it, but my case is moderate or manageable.
- I've got it, and it's really bad.

No matter the conclusion, it is important that you accept it.

Many of you will identify others who are experiencing some, many, or most of the symptoms. It is often easier to see what is happening to others than yourself. You may discover you are more irritated with someone who you believe has one of the diseases but does not recognize it. Remember, what you see in others, may be in you. It disturbs you because deep inside, you know it is impacting you. Perhaps these tendencies are another undiscovered disease. Also, avoid putting all the focus on others, label them, or make light of their difficulties.

How do you determine severity? What if you think you have 100% of the symptoms? It's simple, you have an extreme case. The chapters in the back portion of the book will present more on how to deal with extreme cases or multiple diseases at the same time.

Engaging Others

It is important to involve others. Most of you will naturally engage those closest to you. You will tell them when something is occurring, seems unusual, or feels abnormal. You will ask for their opinion or viewpoint on what they may have noticed. You will compare notes, listen to their experiences, and pay closer attention as you try to figure out what is happening to you.

You may want to enlist the help of a leader whom you highly respect. Some leaders have already identified and utilized a proven few upon whom they rely for advice and support. A board of advisors is another model which leaders find valuable. There may be occasions when a superior, friend, or colleague will open this book and point to specific diseases and inform you of their belief that you have contracted one or more of them.

Are there professionally trained individuals who are familiar with these diseases and their treatment? Not necessarily. At the time of the book's publication, there were none who have been formally trained to specifically address the list of leadership diseases outlined here. These diseases are newly recognized. There has been little time to train or teach professionals to diagnose and treat.

Yet, there are experienced leaders, coaches, mentors, and teachers who will recognize the diseases easily and be able to integrate this information into their methods and approaches. There are many well written books which dive deeply into aspects of the diseases or offer a comprehensive exploration.

Impact & Treatment

If you have determined you may have or do have a disease, it's time to look at the impact it may have on you and your team or organization. Analyze the impact. What are you noticing is happening within your organization or with your people? Maybe there are hidden outcomes which you do not see now but need to realize may happen or are already happening and you are not aware.

Evaluating the impact is a form of risk assessment. How critical are the outcomes to you or your team or organization? To what stage has the disease advanced? How severe is it and how painful? Is there already or will there be damage? The impact is primarily about you, the patient, but we all know that the impact of the illness on you will directly affect those you lead.

Maybe your disease has not advanced significantly, and you want to consider what to do in order to reduce its impact. In considering you next steps, reflect on these questions: What will it cost you in time, energy, and money? Are you willing and capable of making the sacrifice? Is it time to create an exit strategy and learn from your mistakes?

It takes introspection on the leader's part to recognize the disease's status and then plan for the future. A wise person is one who can recognize a personal illness and take steps to address it. We will continue to remind you of the assistance of others in this process of assessing impact and planning treatment.

Remember, people may be afraid to tell you what illnesses they believe you to have. Give them license to be candid. You might give someone a copy of this book and ask for a diagnosis, anonymous or not, offering an opportunity to tell you which diseases they think you have.

One final warning, feedback for you may become an opportunity for people to make inaccurate assessments of you or what is happening in your leadership life. As part of your consideration of their input, assess their motives by asking yourself questions such as these: Are they trying to curry favor? Are they attempting to convince you of something? Are they just praising you for the goodwill it may buy?

At the end of the book, more is presented about implementation and application for recognizing and handling diseases for you and others. This information may be helpful to you in addressing the diseases you have or may encounter. Some of you may want to jump ahead and read these sections before you begin your diagnosis.

Listening Is Key

Most of you have heard and believe that listening to others is critical to the success of a leader. It is a skill and an art. It can be taught and learned. Some have it naturally; others must work at it.

Listening is very important to your analysis of the diseases. Those who know you, work with you, or follow your lead can be the best source of input for you. Listening is how you collect data outside yourself. What do they see, know, and understand about you and the disease? You will need the help of those around you.

As you look at yourself in light of one or more diseases, you may make critical mistakes in your communication. Remember, if you have the disease, it may cloud your judgment, distorting your thinking and making it difficult to effectively communicate. Your fear, apprehension, confusion, anger, and misunderstanding may create conditions causing you to make serious communication mistakes.

A leader can often recover from poor communication by simply listening. An open and calm mind can counterbalance some of the more damaging aspects of a leader's poor or inadequate communication. You can learn more from people if you really listen. When you do not listen, you can overlook great ideas, solutions, and breakthroughs, or worse, you can betray your personal values.

Much has been written on the topic of listening; therefore, I am not going to offer all kinds of advice and techniques on how to be a better listener. But here are a few concepts which are universal.

- Leaders must continuously listen to all stakeholders.
- Leaders who are good listeners foster outcomes.
- Listening can generate understanding of another person's reality and feelings.
- Information, feedback, and data are available if you actively listen.
- Listening is essential; understanding is critical.
- Know there is a time to listen and a time to act.
- Listening without judgment is quite difficult, but very important.
- Ask clarifying questions, control your negative emotions, have an open mind.

I will also make a plug for observation, not interacting, but watching what is going on around you. Pay close attention to how people interact. It might even be something they say about you. In meetings, watch the reactions to you or to a message being given by you or someone else. You never know what you might learn.

Formula for Healthier Leadership

After you scan the list of diseases, you might realize there are three items missing. They are integrity, honesty, and trust. If a disease definition was assigned to each, it would be described as lack of integrity, dishonesty, and not trustworthy.

In my research, I asked:

"What is the worst thing a leader can do?"

The response was often some form of these three:

"A leader must have integrity."

"A leader has to be honest."

"A leader must be trustworthy in the eyes of others."

These frequent responses referred to a leader's negative relationship with any one or all of the three missing virtues presented above.

As I read and listened to my cohort of leadership practitioners talk about these principles, I concluded that a lack of these qualities should not be included in the disease list. It appeared the three were pre-conditions or requirements for a leader who wanted to be leadership healthy. When neglected or seldom practiced, the leader's probability of staying healthy or being a good leader was diminished significantly and shortened the length of time a leader could effectively function as a leader.

Healthcare professionals consistently and constantly advise us to adhere to a formula, a set of rules, or habits for good health. They will say, in order to stay healthy, you need to "Eat right, exercise, and get plenty of rest." Everyone has heard some version of these admonitions. Leaders need to follow similar advice, but the mantra is different. It says, if you want to be a good leader or have a healthier leadership life, **have integrity, be honest, and build trust.**

People want to follow leaders with whom they identify and with whom they have a relationship. Transactions based on integrity, honesty, and trust enhance these relationships. Followers want to respect the person who has power over them. If the one in charge is missing or perceived as lacking an adherence to the formula, their respect, motivation, and enthusiasm to follow that leader are severely damaged or even disappear.

All of us are negatively impacted by not adhering to physical and mental health principles and habits. Leaders who do not follow the leadership health advice of practicing integrity, being honest, and instilling trust, can see adverse results. Diseases may strike quicker, have a greater negative impact, or make recovery more difficult.

What if you experience multiple leadership diseases at the same time, have a severe case, or encounter one after another? Your prognosis may be very serious, disastrous, non-treatable, impossible to recover from, or a total failure, if you have not followed the leadership mantra. The absence of these will magnify your symptoms and impact.

Not following the healthy leadership lifestyle principles may create other unintended consequences. If you violate any of these basic tenets, you give your people permission to do the same or worse. If a leader cannot be trusted, is dishonest, or lacks integrity, why shouldn't everyone else be the same. Mistrust, disrespect, and dishonesty become implanted in your teams, culture, and organization.

Again, the formula is simple, but it is not easy.

Integrity + Honesty + Trust = Healthier Leadership

Circumstances

Not every symptom implies a disease. In the field of medicine, there are injuries. We are quite familiar with them as most of us have had cuts, abrasions, sprains, strains, burns, and broken bones. Most of these happen as accidents which are usually beyond our control. Yet some occur when we are not paying attention or do not understand what might happen.

In leadership, there are circumstances which are conditions connected with or relevant to an event or action. Those circumstances are also beyond our control. Or, similar to injury, they occur when we lack an understanding of or are simply unaware of what is happening around us.

It is important to distinguish between a circumstance and a disease as it applies to leadership. A circumstance can be a sudden event, a situation, an incident, or an accident. It is usually done to you or impacts you, either directly or indirectly.

A leadership disease derives from you, or something to which you have been exposed. It usually occurs because of something you are doing or not doing. A leadership disease usually has a gradual onset. Seldom does it happen all at once. It is there, lingering or getting worse. Your awareness of it may happen due to an incident or event, but it has already been there for a while.

Circumstances may be when a new player, who is better or different than you, enters the scene. That person could emerge due to the actions of others. There could be a shift within the economy, law, technology, or culture. Conditions might change for the environment, finances, or politics. Circumstances can be new information or a scientific discovery. These changes may be traumatic or catastrophic, perhaps generating a crisis. Normally, you are not in control of any of these.

Sometimes it is quite difficult to distinguish between an injury and a disease. You might think that a person has betrayed you (injury), but you picked them (disease). It might be an unseen report (injury), but you did not pay attention to it (disease). Funding has changed, a legal precedent was set, or your competitor became more successful. Yes, those are circumstances, but they are also trends and regular occurrences for which you did not account.

It may be difficult to see the difference, but do not allow a circumstance to become an excuse for your illness. It is not a way to escape your role, avoid your responsibility, or lay blame. Evaluating and analyzing circumstances are part of your diagnostic process. As it has been said earlier, everyone encounters diseases and gets sick. Also, everyone gets injured at some point. A leader needs to understand the difference.

What's Ailing You

You likely have been given much to consider already and are intrigued to take a look at the diseases. In many ways this book is a set of tools designed to help you think and reflect. Now it's time to look at the diseases and assess your condition from the past, currently, and into the future.

Face these potential ailments as you would any disease. Become aware, educate yourself, and engage the help of knowledgeable people who can help you. Understand how the disease is impacting you, plan for treatment, and implement it. Determine if you are getting better or worse and adjust appropriately.

Do not be afraid. We all become ill. Leaders become leadersick. What is important is how you confront it and how you handle it. Because we know that **when leaders get better, we all get better**, and isn't that what everyone wants?

GUIDE TO LEADERSHIP DISEASES

The central portion of this book includes the list of 28 leadership diseases. Each disease has a chapter dedicated to it and information presented follows the same format within each chapter. Following the explanation of the format are Helpful Tips for the Reader. It will be quite valuable for you to **review that section** before you take a deep dive into each disease.

As noted above, the leadership diseases are organized into five groups for easier reference.

GROUP A - SELF
What you understand about yourself.
Self-perception, self-awareness.

GROUP B - CAPACITY
What your load is.
Balance, boundaries, limitations.

GROUP C - STYLE
How you address your role.
Methods, philosophy, framework.

GROUP D - ASSIGNMENT
Who does the work.
Allocation, designation, responsibilities.

GROUP E - PEOPLE
How you treat those you lead.
Interactions, relationships.

 LeadersickBook.com/index-of-diseases/

Disease Chapter Format

Each disease chapter is presented using the same format, similar to those used in medical publications when depicting diseases.

The chapter will begin with a classification section to provide general information and then followed by three checklists:

- Symptoms - Signs & Causes
- Impact - Risk Factors, Stages & Outcomes
- Treatment - Remedy, Prevention & Control

The chapter structure is designed to assist the reader in understanding the dynamics of the disease and determining how each may apply. Each checklist section heading is accompanied by a clarifying question to help you grasp how the statement fits and shapes your analysis.

Classification

Name: Some disease names are understood visually, and some are more easily grasped auditorily. A disease may have a nickname or shortened version for easier reference.

Pronunciation: A phonetic spelling is provided for each disease name to demonstrate a way in which it may be spoken. *Do not get stuck on the pronunciation.* If you want to hear it, visit LeadersickBook.com/pronunciations/ to listen to the pronunciation.

Definition: A brief description provides a summary explanation for each disease.

Derivation: Each name was originated using abbreviated, modified, or common words combined with some medical suffixes or prefixes.

Interchangeable Words: In some of the diseases, it may be helpful for readers to substitute words which are more applicable to their situation and circumstances. As we mentioned in the first part of the book, the word **goal** might be more appropriately considered as vision, mission, objective, task, or project. **Team** might be called group, organization, board, committee, class, division, section, squad, or crew.

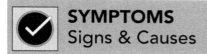

SYMPTOMS
Signs & Causes

Are you experiencing now or in the past any of these? Does it apply to you?

A healthcare professional would usually begin with, "What's going on? How are you feeling? What are you experiencing?" A process is being followed to assess your condition and determine your wellbeing. Similar questions are being asked here. "What is occurring? What conditions exist within your groups, teams, units, or organizations?"

Statements are presented as choices for you to select ones which are clearly true, perhaps, partially correct, or somewhat accurate. They are presented in **first person** to make them more relevant to you. Not all statements will apply and may be in an area where you have no experience, have never worked, or have ever considered. Statements in this checklist derive from two perspectives.

Internal is what comes directly from the leader or is inside each of us. We often call this self-talk or the voice inside your head. You either **feel or believe** something OR **tell yourself or think** something. Internal can also be your actions when you **say or do** something. As a leader, your behaviors are generated from your head, your heart, or your soul. When you review the Symptom statements, ask yourself, "Which statements belong to me?"

External is when we scan the landscape seeking or discovering what other people feel, believe, think, or do. We acquire input through observation, listening, and reading. We notice what people **say** and how they **act**. We interpret from both their verbal and non-verbal cues.

Input may come when others tell you about what they have witnessed. External information is sometimes sought but may also just arrive uninvited. No matter when or how it comes, consider the source's credibility and motives. Is the information candid and honest? Occasionally, someone may even talk to you about you. When this happens, pay close attention. It could be very helpful.

A simpler and more personal version of how to review each statement in the Symptoms Checklist may be:

- Is it related to me? How I see me.
- Is it relevant to others? How I see others.
- Is it relevant to the circumstance? How I see the world.

For those readers who do not worry about what others think of them or may challenge with "I don't know what others think," concentrate on your perceptions and do not get entangled in the external data. Don't overthink it.

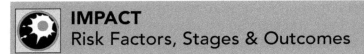

IMPACT
Risk Factors, Stages & Outcomes

What has already happened or might occur?

This section deals with outcomes and impact upon you, your people, or your organization. It is a third person perspective, the impressions of one who is observing from the outside. Each statement is written in present tense but can be applied to the past (already experienced it), present (is happening now or very recently), and future (could occur).

The diagnosis may help you understand how seriously the disease may be hitting you. It could indicate the intensity of the illness, or what phase you are entering or exiting. It may also help pinpoint specific aspects of the disease as it impacts you. It may be like reading the warning label or hearing a healthcare professional say, "You may experience body aches, fever, headache, nausea, diarrhea, shortness of breath, dizziness, loss of feeling in your limbs . . ."; the list goes on forever.

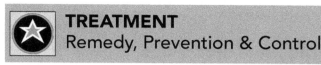

TREATMENT
Remedy, Prevention & Control

What strategies might work for you? What are you committing to do?

These statements are your choices for healing or managing the disease. Each is powered by a verb meaning you can act. Some are passive recommendations for you to consider, realize, listen, assess, analyze, and thoughtfully consider. Permanent or significant change does not occur until you truly understand, think, believe, and act differently.

The checklist in this section is not an all-inclusive or exhaustive one. You may find that some treatment modalities for one disease might find success with a different one. Treatment suggestions may come from others as you talk about your disease and learn how they handled their healing.

As you read the list, you may combine a couple of different thoughts or think of a new idea to try. Some may work; others may not. It's like finding the right medical therapy, treatment, or medication which works for you. It is often trial and error until the correct remedy is identified.

It was not repeated in every Treatment section, but mentors, coaches, and counselors can have a great impact on you. We all need people with whom we can build a therapeutic relationship. We all need someone who listens, teaches, prescribes, and suggests steps we can take to become better.

NOTES
Observations, Reflections & Conclusions

What were our thoughts? What were yours?

This section includes brief remarks or comments which may enhance your understanding and analysis of the disease, refer, or connect to other diseases, or offer points for discussion and interaction.

This area is also an excellent place to add your personal notations about what is on your mind as you have reviewed a disease. Your analysis may have created questions or made you think of items missing from a checklist. You might jot a note about something you noticed or a conclusion you have reached.

 Visit LeadersickBook.com/reader-feedback/ to share your thoughts. Your comments may be helpful to others as they consider the diseases.

Helpful Tips for The Reader

It is strongly recommended that you review the Helpful Tips (bold) section before you dive into the diseases. It will help your understanding, application, and analysis of each disease.

Using the Checklists

Use this publication as a workbook. As you review each checklist, mark items which are relevant to your leadership health. **Check all which apply** to you (or the person you are analyzing). Do not be overly cautious. Make notes, underline, and highlight as you review each checklist. Look for patterns. Consider your thoughts as you review. You may gain some great insights as you simply determine your status with each disease.

Reader's Perspective

The checklist items are written in a way for you to make the statement more personal. Inserting yourself into the statement may help it feel real. Ask yourself, does this statement have any form of truth within it? Is it from long ago, or is it more recent? Is it present now? Is it repetitive or more occasional? Is it growing or shrinking?

Language Form

Slang and contractions are used periodically to more clearly depict how people think and what they hear from their inner voice. Common phrases or cultural references may be used to better trigger matching thoughts.

Multiple Items

Some items in the checklists may seem repetitive because leaders hear, see, think, or believe in different ways. One phrase may resonate with you, and a similar one may not. Slight nuances may make a difference to the reader. Multiple affirmations, which seem the same, may lead to a stronger recognition of a contracted disease.

Checklist Order

The checklist statements are not presented in any specific order. They are intentionally not grouped, prioritized, sequenced, or weighted. The importance or significance of each statement will vary by a leader's perceptions, experiences, and values.

Interchangeable Words

In some of the disease chapters you are offered a variety of word choices that may be substituted or seem more fitting. Based on how you think or the language used in your organization or culture, certain words are more appropriate or have a common meaning. One leader may speak of projects while another talks about programs or products. One might describe a behavior as terrible while another may call it unacceptable or harmful. Feel free to substitute interchangeable words to better fit your situation or circumstances.

Considerations for Analysis

It may be difficult to think about each of the statements in light of multiple leadership roles. You can either think about your leadership as a whole, or you can think about one specific entity and analyze from that point of view. Most of us do not lead in completely different ways across settings and situations.

Self   Assignment

Style   Capacity   People

LEADERSICK DISEASES

DISEASE GROUPINGS

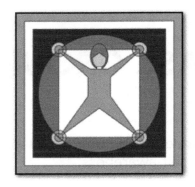

A. SELF

What you understand about yourself. Self-perception, self-awareness.

Perception is how we view our reality and how that view helps us interpret the world around us. Self-perception is an image we hold about ourselves, our traits, and the judgments we make about those traits. Self-awareness is the capacity to look inward and understand our own feelings, emotions, stressors, and personality. These key understandings play a critical role in influencing our judgments, decisions, and interactions.

A1. Egomegaly

PRONUNCIATION: ee'-goh-meh'-guh-lee

DEFINITION: Big or over enlarged ego. You are right about everything. You are smarter and better.

DERIVATION: **Eg** = ego + **ormegaly** = enlargement

 SYMPTOMS
Signs & Causes

Are you experiencing any of these now or in the past? Which apply to you?

❑ People say, "You are not listening to me" or "You don't listen to me."

❑ You believe the organization you lead could not survive without you.

❑ You think you know everything (or nearly everything).

❑ You seldom include others in decisions or analysis.

❑ You ascribe to the *great person theory*, and that is you.

❑ You like it when people believe you are the best, most experienced, or most successful.

❑ You take all the credit, or you feel you deserve all the credit when something positive happens.

❑ You are in love with your ideas. They are the best.

❑ You select people for your team who think you are great (or at least tell you that).

❑ People think or say it's all about you.

❑ You think any or all of these: "I can have it all, I know it all, or I can be anything I want to be."

❑ No one questions your opinions, thoughts, or directives.

❑ You have been told you are not a good listener.

❑ You believe you have all the answers.

❑ Some people might describe you as arrogant.

❑ You create projects which are very comfortable for you or highlight your skills and talent.

❑ People say that you love to have the spotlight on you.

❑ You believe that all you have and all you have achieved are because of you.

❑ Everyone agrees with you and tells you your ideas are great.

❑ You have been told that you surround yourself with *yes-people*.

❑ You tell people and believe you are right about everything.

❑ You believe that results are primarily because of your efforts.

❑ People talk about servant leadership and you either don't know what they are talking about, or you think it's a load of manure.

❏ You become a mentor because you know how to turn someone into another you.

❏ You think or say, "There are two opinions, one is mine and the other is incorrect."

❏ You are proud of being overly confident.

❏ You truly believe you are infallible, mistake proof (maybe a small one now and then).

❏ You want to be known as the expert on everything.

❏ You don't realize when others have helped or supported you (sometimes doing some or all of the work).

❏ Everyone waits for you to act first, speak first, or make the first move.

❏ You think this disease is stupid and none of it applies to you.

⚙ IMPACT
Risk Factors, Stages & Outcomes

What has already happened or might occur?

❏ People are afraid to ask you questions.

❏ Some people realize that you are pretending to be an expert.

❏ You seldom get the truth about a situation when it includes you.

❏ You have people who try to prove you wrong.

❏ New ideas are seldom created or presented, particularly to you.

❏ You buy into the hype that you are smarter and better than all others.

❏ People do not warn you or your people of possible errors or mistakes.

❏ People give you what they think you want, not what you may need.

❏ There is little trust between you and those who follow you.

❏ People feel that no matter their effort, it will not be good enough for you.

❏ People wonder why they should exert any effort when all the credit goes to you.

❏ People feel like they will never be good enough or ever as good as you.

❏ Decision making is poor with less-than-optimal results.

❏ People view your dominating and upstaging as bigfooting.

❏ There is no license to be honest or disagree with you.

❏ People assume you know more or are smarter than others, so there is no reason to learn.

❏ People will not offer their leadership because you will always be in charge.

❏ You lose highly talented and supremely motivated people who want a leadership role similar to yours.

❏ People do not want to work with you because of your reputation.

❏ You do not look for people who may be smarter than you or you ignore them when you see them.

❏ Without having good or great people, you cannot get as much done.

❏ People will only do what they think will please you or do it the way you would.

- [ ] You are seen as being narcissistic or having a superiority complex.
- [ ] Some people will sabotage your efforts or try to make you look bad.

 TREATMENT
Remedy, Prevention & Control

What strategies might work for you? What are you committing to do?

- [ ] Realize and accept that you are not always right and do not know everything.
- [ ] Change your approach to decision making by involving others.
- [ ] Listen and seek to understand what someone is explaining.
- [ ] Have an open conversation about yourself with someone you trust and who will be honest with you.
- [ ] Talk with people who want to help make you a better person.
- [ ] Publicly acknowledge what you don't know. Make it a big deal.
- [ ] Sit down, dress more casually, or stand back when you are talking with people.
- [ ] When someone is candid with you about you, say, "I hear you and appreciate your feedback."
- [ ] Ask someone to tell you something you need to hear, but they have been afraid to say.
- [ ] Do not penalize or punish people who are honest with you about you.

❑ Tell yourself that it is unrealistic to know everything. There is always more to know.

❑ Set conditions for a person to discreetly call you out or challenge you, and then give that person permission to do it.

❑ Recognize and thank those who help you achieve or do the work on your behalf.

❑ If you are told something about yourself which catches you off guard, tell them, "Let me think about what you said." Then think about it and get back to them.

❑ Remind yourself that it is not all about you and what you can gain.

❑ Ask someone to tell you something you do not want to hear about yourself.

❑ Put the needs of others ahead of your own.

❑ When you hear something unsettling about yourself, pour yourself a cold one (or a hot one) and seriously consider what was said.

❑ Stop making things up when you really don't know. (Be honest; you know when you are doing it.)

❑ Tell stories of how someone challenged you and how it made a positive impact on you.

❑ Incorporate the ideas, perspectives, and expertise of your people.

❑ Ask others to help you improve or overcome a problem that your ego created.

❑ Promote or publicly recognize someone who disagrees, challenges, or questions you.

❑ Before you begin anything, remind yourself that you don't know or understand everything.

❏ Draw experts in to help.

❏ Set your ego aside and listen to someone in the bottom of your organization.

❏ Realize your size, stature, or appearance are intimidating and find ways to tone them down.

❏ Look at leaders you admire (someone you see as incredibly talented and amazingly accomplished) and compare yourself honestly. Or ask someone to offer their analysis.

❏ Understand, believe, and practice that no one person is bigger than the team, group, or organization.

❏ Become a reflective or active listener.

❏ Volunteer or spend time with people who are known to be humble or are less fortunate.

NOTES
Observations, Reflections & Conclusions

• Related diseases are Nayopening (p. 49) and Hypermanagitis (p. 148)

• People with big egos may not truly be aware they have one.

• Learning that one has a large ego may be a very difficult process for the one who has it and the one who is trying to help with the discovery.

• However small or great our influence or power is, we tend to take pride in it and are reluctant to let it go.

A2. CREDITNOMEXIA

PRONUNCIATION: kred'-it-no-meks'-ee-uh

DEFINITION: Do not give enough credit to self for accomplishments. Do not understand your capabilities. Overly humble; do not want to appear as taking credit away from others.

DERIVATION: **CREDIT** + **NO** + to **ME** + e**XIA** = a condition or pathology

SYMPTOMS
Signs & Causes

Are you experiencing any of these now or in the past? Which apply to you?

- ❏ When praise is given to you, you reject it or are embarrassed.

- ❏ You believe being humble is a required personal value.

- ❏ You think it's best to give others all the credit without recognizing you were part.

- ❏ After completion of a project, you focus on what did not go well or what could have been better.

- ❏ You don't want people to think you are bragging.

❏ When asked about your background, you provide a vague and limited explanation.

❏ You think your contributions or accomplishments are not that significant.

❏ After you have explained something from your past, you hear "I didn't know that about you."

❏ You downplay the importance of what you have done.

❏ You believe presenting facts about your accomplishments is not necessary.

❏ You over-acknowledge or dwell on your mistakes and missteps.

❏ You were taught or told as you grew up to not talk about yourself too much.

❏ You believe that other leaders will hear about your accomplishments without your telling them.

❏ When you introduce yourself, you omit your title and make no reference to your leadership roles.

❏ Your faith teaches that being humble is important.

❏ You are seen as a nice person, or you come from a culture which taught you to be nice to others.

❏ When you consider talking about yourself, your inner voice says, "Don't say much."

❏ You think being reserved may be an excuse to cover your apprehension to talk about yourself.

❏ When you are sharing your background, people who know you tell others what you have forgotten to mention.

❏ You often deflect compliments.

❏ You hear others say to you, "You realize that was a compliment."

❑ No matter how well things turn out, you still notice all the misses.

❑ You dwell on opportunities you have missed.

 IMPACT
Risk Factors, Stages & Outcomes

What has already happened or might occur?

❑ People must guess or make assumptions about your capabilities.

❑ You deprive others of your expertise.

❑ People are irritated later when they learn that you have withheld expertise or skills from them.

❑ People see you as weak because they believe you do not have much to offer.

❑ Others undervalue your leadership.

❑ Others do not realize what you did or know the contribution you made.

❑ People interpret your being humble as lack of confidence or self-doubt.

❑ You lose opportunities to leverage your reputation in order to accomplish something important to you.

❑ Others think, if you cannot present your abilities and strengths, how do you expect them to.

❑ People lose faith in you and do not trust your abilities.

❑ People feel insecure with you as a leader who seems weak rather than humble.

❑ People decide to not talk about their attributes because they think it might make you look bad.

❑ People wonder if your leadership had anything to do with a success or victory.

❏ Your behavior is interpreted as overly vulnerable.

❏ Others share little about themselves, believing you think it is unimportant.

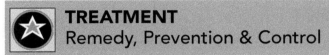

TREATMENT
Remedy, Prevention & Control

What strategies might work for you? What are you committing to do?

❏ Facts are facts. State what is factual about yourself.

❏ Face your fear; tell yourself that you can do it.

❏ Share more about yourself so others feel free to do the same.

❏ Talk about some of your shortcomings or challenges to offset your sharing of your extensive background.

❏ Each week, share one or two highlights from your past seven days with someone.

❏ Talk about some of your leadership roles in order to help people understand your capabilities and passions.

❏ Ask others which of your strengths and abilities help them.

❏ Explore the true meaning of pride and humility.

❏ Recognize that leaving a legacy through relationship influence is an achievement in itself.

❏ Make a timeline for yourself of what you have accomplished in your leadership roles.

❏ Realize that your deference to achievement recognition does not downplay the importance of personal fulfillment.

❏ Watch how others convey their accomplishments without sounding boastful.

❑ Realize many others may view you as more powerful, effective, and influential than you think you are.

❑ Serve as a role model for how to accurately present yourself.

❑ Maintain a balance between being too humble and feeling self-important.

❑ Ask others to tell you what they think are your major accomplishments and what that means.

❑ Be the first to openly talk about self, so others will do the same.

❑ When recognized for an achievement, remind yourself you earned it, people want to show appreciation, and they want you to take time to enjoy it.

❑ Acknowledge your vulnerabilities and submit to accountability to lessen the trap of pride.

❑ Accurately portray the balance between how your leadership shaped the results and how your team contributed.

❑ Remind yourself that true fulfillment is cherished and valued when you understand it's an important part of your leadership journey.

❑ Annually make a list of all your accomplishments for the past 12 months; include everything.

❑ Share that list with people who are close to you and ask for their feedback, input, and validation.

❑ Give yourself credit and see how it feels. Just do it.

NOTES
Observations, Reflections & Conclusions

• Having a low opinion of oneself can translate into or be seen as an unwillingness to take care of self.

- There are multiple facets to this ailment: you have talent and do not share it; you do not have confidence; or you do not understand your talents and expertise.

- You may have an overlap with UNREFLECTHABITIS (p. 66).

- Note the significant difference between saying "I scored 100% correctly on the test," versus "Hey, hey, hey! Look at me! I'm the smartest in the class! I scored 100."

- "Humility is not thinking less of yourself, it's thinking of yourself less." (Rick Warren)

A3. NAYOPENING

PRONUNCIATION: nay-op'-e-ning

DEFINITION: You are unapproachable, difficult to access. Perceived as too important, too busy.

DERIVATION: **NAY** = no + **OPENING**

SYMPTOMS
Signs & Causes

Are you experiencing any of these now or in the past? Which apply to you?

❏ You do not take calls, or your calls are screened.

❏ People say you are very difficult to reach.

❏ You do not return calls in a timely manner. You are too busy or want people to think so.

❏ You believe that the only people who really have something to offer to you are your peers.

❏ You do not respond to many of the text messages and emails you receive.

❏ When you are in, the door to your office is usually closed.

❑ You try to ignore people who are attempting to get your attention.

❑ There is a gatekeeper outside your workspace who inspects and deflects requests to access you.

❑ People hesitate, rethink, or drop approaching you.

❑ People say, "Good luck getting hold of that person."

❑ You believe it just natural and inevitable to live the maxim of "It's lonely at the top."

❑ You consider what people bring to you as petty, small, or trivial, and you let them know it.

❑ You keep your camera turned off most of the time on video calls.

❑ People stop asking you to join organizations or boards.

❑ Sending a quick text or short email to someone seems a waste of your time.

❑ You have someone sort through your emails to determine which ones should be answered.

❑ When you are with those you know, you form a tight circle signaling "There is no space for anyone else."

❑ People have quit approaching you with anything, even the little things.

❑ You have feelings of being lonely or isolated.

❑ You feel like your network has become a small, tight group.

❑ It appears to others there is nothing you need or want.

❑ You check your email, and you have no new emails except those which are auto reply.

❑ When a project (you would really enjoy or have much to offer) arises, no one considers asking you.

❑ People are afraid to ask you questions.

❑ You tell people that you do not do video calls.

❑ People describe you as having a coat of armor around you.

❑ Opening remarks from others begin with "I know you're really busy" or "I hate to bother you."

IMPACT
Risk Factors, Stages & Outcomes

What has already happened or might occur?

❑ You seldom hear directly about opportunities.

❑ New ideas are not brought to you very often.

❑ You are not asked to speak to groups or classes.

❑ Some people just give up trying to reach you.

❑ No one shares information about you because no one knows what it would be.

❑ People avoid or stay away from you.

❑ You become isolated and lonely.

❑ You are not invited to events.

❑ You are seen as not needing or seeking anything.

❑ People accept your non-verbal messages and quit trying to approach you.

❑ You get little opportunity to talk things over with others.

❑ People are not sure if you are a good speaker or storyteller because they have never talked with you.

❑ People think you are playing a game of "Look at me, I am busier than you."

❑ No one is following you because you are so separated from everything.

❑ People think it is a waste of time to approach you.

❑ Your phone calls diminish significantly.

❑ Your reputation becomes "You think you are more important than the rest of us."

❑ People interpret your behaviors as you are so strong you do not need anything.

❑ People may see you at the top and think you are stuck there or will remain there forever.

❑ People may see no reason to hitch their fortune to a star that is out of reach or dimming.

❑ People keeping asking and seeking from you, but they become more frustrated and irritated.

★ TREATMENT
Remedy, Prevention & Control

What strategies might work for you? What are you committing to do?

❑ Spend time with the ones who think highly of you and can overlook when you are being a jerk.

❑ Respond with "I have put you on my list of things to do," then follow up soon.

❑ Admit you do not know something and are open to learning.

❑ When standing or sitting with a group of people, make sure there is open space for others to join.

❑ Let people know quickly that you are *not* too busy to respond to them or to an issue.

❑ Ask people to tell you what they need from you.

❑ If they are not clear, ask questions.

❑ Respond with a date or time when you can get to someone. Let them know they are important.

❏ Make more time for the ones you trust and will hold in confidence what you say.

❏ Ask for help in finding the answer to a problem.

❏ Perform a menial task with someone.

❏ Control your need to be busy by screening tasks with "I will do _____ in order to get to my goal of _____."

❏ When busy, get the attention of someone by giving a non-verbal signal that you want to talk.

❏ Let schools, classes, clubs, and groups know you are available to be a speaker or presenter.

❏ Prior to announcing your availability, read a book or take a class or course in how to be a good speaker.

❏ Think through your personal story to prepare your thoughts on what you have learned and advice you would give.

❏ Manage expectations by being careful how and when you respond.

❏ Do not show irritation when people begin to reconnect with you.

 NOTES
Observations, Reflections & Conclusions

• Can be related to Supraperfektus (p. 60) or Dynamopexy (p. 54).

• May be self-inflicted, meaning you are creating this reality, or it may be the perception of others.

• Remember, if you become isolated, you could have no one to lead. It is difficult to call yourself a leader when you have nobody following your leadership.

A4. Dynamopexy

Pronunciation: dai'-nuh-mo-peks'-ee

Definition: Relies on personal power, stature, and reputation.

Derivation: **DYNAMO** = power, strength + **PEXY** = fixation.

✓ SYMPTOMS
Signs & Causes

Are you experiencing any of these now or in the past? Which apply to you?

- ❏ People will describe you as a leader who *likes to throw your weight around.*

- ❏ You get rid of people easily.

- ❏ You believe it is good for people to have a little (or a lot of) fear of you.

- ❏ Some people refer to you as *The Hammer, Slave Driver*, or another harsh descriptor.

- ❏ When you are asked why, your answer is often, "Because I said so."

- ❏ You believe you are of great value to the organization.

- ❏ You realize that your positions create power for you.

❑ You do not share your decisions with others until necessary.

❑ You love to win and hate to lose.

❑ You have a very impressive office.

❑ You believe that people need to work their way up because that's what you did.

❑ You know threats are a good way to motivate people.

❑ You have been told that you are condescending, or you have felt that way at times.

❑ You intentionally withhold information from time to time.

❑ You get upset if someone introduces you but does not roll out your credentials strongly enough.

❑ You believe in the statement, "When you know more than others, you have more power."

❑ You like the concept of sanctions.

❑ You enjoy telling stories where you are the hero.

❑ You *water down* titles or provide none when you introduce others.

❑ You generally rely on the old way of doing things.

❑ You have a space (or more than one) where you display the symbols of your success.

❑ Someone wrote on the lunchroom wall, "_____ is a tyrant!" And your name was in the blank.

❑ You believe punishment is the best way to handle people problems.

❑ You enjoy books and movies about people who conquered, triumphed, won, dominated.

❑ It irritates you when people do not know who you are.

❑ People see you as capitalizing on other's mistakes, misfortunes, and problems.

❑ You believe that coercion is just a tool for getting things done.

❑ You think or hear yourself saying, "If it weren't for me . . . ."

❑ You are known to take advantage of your colleagues.

❑ You believe in the (other) Golden Rule, "He (or she) who has the gold, makes the rules."

❑ People feel they cannot win around you.

IMPACT
Risk Factors, Stages & Outcomes

What has already happened or might occur?

❑ Your people are maliciously obedient.

❑ Your people do not like or are worn down by how you leverage power to motivate them.

❑ People do not do their best because they know it would be bad to outshine you.

❑ People are very disappointed by not receiving praise for what they achieve.

❑ If some people get an opportunity, they stick it to you.

❑ No one wants to challenge what you hold dear: power, stature, and reputation.

❑ People believe you don't trust others.

❑ People believe you do not want anyone else to have power.

❑ People leave to get away from you.

❑ People do not want others to know they are following a tyrannical leader.

❑ Some people are rooting for you to take a big fall.

❑ People view you as self-absorbed.

❑ Some people think you are hiding behind your symbols of power.

❑ People believe you think you are better than they are and don't respect them.

❑ People see a clear divide between them and you or what you have achieved.

❑ People believe you could hurt or even destroy the organization.

❑ You lose your followership which reduces your power.

❑ Some people will put their efforts into sabotaging yours.

❑ You are not respected by others.

❑ People who do not value power, stature, or reputation think you're an ass.

❑ Some people believe doing it your way does not work any longer.

❑ The coercive tactics of fear or force become less effective over time.

❑ People think your efforts are focused on looking good, impressive, and successful.

❑ People believe your formula for success does not include them.

❑ People think you have a superiority complex.

❑ People reduce their efforts knowing they will never achieve what you have nor share in it.

TREATMENT
Remedy, Prevention & Control

What strategies might work for you? What are you committing to do?

❏ Share your power by involving them in important decision making.

❏ Learn about positive motivational techniques and try them.

❏ Make a list of the positive aspects of your power, stature, and reputation.

❏ Then, make a list of all the negative parts of your power, stature, and reputation.

❏ Display memorabilia which have stories of important values about the organization, not just you.

❏ Publicly share recognition and bestow accolades on others who were part of the effort.

❏ Reduce the number of awards and recognitions on display, keeping only the ones which are most important to you.

❏ Help others get access to your network of people.

❏ Post awards and recognitions of others in public places while replacing the ones about you.

❏ Change your title to something that does not sound traditionally powerful.

❏ Find the positives in any type of introduction made about you.

❏ Explore what role fear and control play in this disease. A therapist or counselor may help.

❏ Connect people to resources to which you have access.

❏ Allow people to share or "piggyback" off your power, stature, and reputation.

❏ Take pictures of your awards for your personal memories, and then get rid of them.

❏ Inspire people with stories of how you got to your level of leadership without bragging.

❏ Treat people with respect and courtesy.

❏ Make a list of what each person has to offer and let each person know you are aware and appreciate it.

❏ Take a look at what symbols of power around you have become ineffective or are inappropriate.

❏ Build relationships where not only you gain, but others experience benefit.

❏ Stop making excuses for why you flaunt your power, stature, and reputation.

NOTES
Observations, Reflections & Conclusions

• There is significant correlation between EGOMEGALY (p. 36) and DYNAMOPEXY (p. 54).

A5. SUPRAPERFEKTUS

PRONUNCIATION: su'-pruh-per-fek'-tuhs

DEFINITION: Thinks a leader (meaning you) must be perfect, most knowledgeable, smartest.

DERIVATION: **SUPRA** = above, excessive + **PERFEK** = perfect + **TUS** = provided with

 SYMPTOMS
Signs & Causes

Are you experiencing any of these now or in the past? Which apply to you?

❏ You believe that leaders should not make mistakes.

❏ You do not share how you feel or what you think because you could be judged or seen as weak, doubting, and unsure.

❏ You expect that you should know what to do or to have the answers all the time.

❏ You believe that you must not fail. You must not make a mistake.

❏ You do not like to acknowledge when you do something wrong.

❑ You take great pride in what you do.

❑ You think people expect you to know the most and be the best.

❑ Often you are highly concerned that you will not get the correct results.

❑ You know you are a role model and are held to a much higher standard.

❑ You are often fearful you might or are going to fail.

❑ You secretly hope other people will screw up, thus taking the focus off you. Actually, you sometimes relish it.

❑ You think your people count on you to know more than anyone else.

❑ Your people say things like: "We are counting on you," "Don't make the wrong decision," "We know you won't lead us astray," and you affirm it by your silence or say "Yes, that's right."

❑ You believe leaders should see all, know all, do all.

❑ People tell you it will not happen to you, you are invincible, and you believe them.

❑ Everyone is counting on you to not make a mistake and damage those who count on your leadership.

❑ You believe that a leader should not show vulnerability.

❑ You believe leaders should be extraordinarily confident, charge forward, and never retreat.

❑ You often worry about not doing it right or not doing the right thing.

❑ You believe there could be dire circumstances if you make a mistake.

❑ You never want people to see you sweat.

❑ You think it is important that you fix everything.

❑ You want to be seen as the best.

❑ You believe leaders must know everything about everything.

IMPACT
Risk Factors, Stages & Outcomes

What has already happened or might occur?

❑ People make more mistakes thinking you like it when they do so, because it makes you look good.

❑ When everything is not perfect, people think you have let them down or withheld information.

❑ You do not admit you are wrong, so you hold on to decisions even when they are not working.

❑ Your dysfunctional beliefs of being perfect damage your ability to be effective.

❑ You take risky actions believing failure cannot happen to you.

❑ You get very upset with yourself when you make a mistake.

❑ Because you expect yourself to be perfect, you expect the same of everyone else, or they think you do.

❑ You surround yourself with people who have a higher propensity to not be perfect.

❑ You put excessive effort into everything, sapping your energy and stamina.

❑ You burn out trying to maintain your unrealistic standard of perfection.

❑ You do not take risky action because you fear failure.

❏ You are so careful to not do something wrong, you limit your actions and risk taking.

❏ No one helps you because they believe you do not need it, do not expect it, or will not accept it.

❏ People think your inability to admit mistakes is a character flaw.

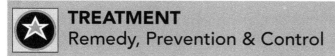

TREATMENT
Remedy, Prevention & Control

What strategies might work for you? What are you committing to do?

❏ Realize that success exists in a process or a system, not just in a person.

❏ Understand that vulnerability is a strength, not a weakness.

❏ Tell yourself regularly that it is OK to make mistakes. That is how we learn and grow.

❏ Make a list of the times you failed or made a mistake, and how it resulted in a positive outcome.

❏ Ask yourself "What is the worst thing that could happen if I am not perfect." Can you live with that outcome?

❏ Read about the mistakes and failures of other leaders where great good or even rewards came as a result.

❏ Convince yourself that leaders (including yourself) are humans, and humans make mistakes.

❏ Publicly announce an error and ask people how they interpreted your action(s).

❏ Admit your mistakes and ask for help.

❑ Analyze the *why* of an imperfect action and learn from it. Model the behavior to others.

❑ Value your qualities of resilience and fortitude in overcoming a challenge.

❑ Search through your past for a time when you were not perfect. Analyze how that experience contributed to your fear of failure.

❑ Realize that failure and major mistakes are a real possibility and natural part learning and growing.

❑ When moving into uncharted territory, realize there is a high probability that perfection may not be attainable.

❑ If the reaction to the announcement of a mistake is negative, ask key people what you could have done differently when revealing your mistake.

❑ Take calculated risks despite the uncertainty that awaits.

❑ Realize when you are not perfect and make mistakes, others may be more willing to step up and offer their help.

❑ Realize that most people do not expect you to know everything.

❑ Communicate that what occurred in an error is a lesson learned and move on.

❑ Focus on your strengths. Quit going in a million different directions.

❑ Look at mistakes as learning opportunities. Review the process that failed, not the person.

❑ Rather than you take the lead, assign responsibilities, and empower others to use their skills and talents to address a specific problem.

NOTES
Observations, Reflections & Conclusions

- Often related to BCT (Blamcritonomy) (p. 178) and Otraperfektus (p. 172).

- There are nuanced differences between Supraperfektus (p. 60) and Egomegaly (p. 36).

- Being open and honest when declaring your errors makes you authentic, and people may have more trust in you.

A6. Noreflecthabitis

Pronunciation: noh'-ree-flek'-tuh-bai'-tuhs

Definition: Not taking time to reflect, rest, and grow. No time for self.

Derivation: **NO** = no + **REFLECT**ing + **HABITIS** = mode of life, habit, or appearance

SYMPTOMS
Signs & Causes

Are you experiencing any of these now or in the past? Which apply to you?

- ❏ You never or seldom take or make the time for yourself.
- ❏ You believe that your faith or belief system tells you to never rest.
- ❏ You do not ask for help or allow yourself to be helped.
- ❏ You have no idea what the term *self-care* means.
- ❏ When on vacation or away, you are constantly calling back and checking email.
- ❏ You have pride in your incredible work ethic and determination to always work hard.

❑ You feel isolated or isolate yourself.

❑ You believe if the leader slows down or rests, everyone else will too.

❑ You have a ton of excuses as to why you don't have time for yourself.

❑ You believe the leader should be the person who puts out the most effort.

❑ You do not schedule in or set time aside to think or reflect.

❑ You think it is a compliment when someone says you are so busy you have no time for yourself.

❑ When you have down time, you get sick or are exhausted.

❑ People would be shocked if you took the time to sit and just talk about nothing.

❑ You have a difficult time doing nothing.

❑ You believe if it's not part of your leadership responsibilities, it's not important.

❑ You know you are too busy to read or study anything.

❑ It has been a long time since you spent any time with your advisors and mentors.

❑ You believe that idle time is a waste of time.

❑ When asked to describe what is on the walls in one of the rooms in your home, you can't recall.

❑ You quickly cancel anything that is not directly related to your responsibilities.

❑ You believe everything is important or urgent.

❑ Getting things done always takes precedence over time for self.

- [ ] You have noticed your energy is down, your intensity lower.
- [ ] It feels like you cannot turn off your brain.
- [ ] You truly believe that sacrificing yourself is part of leadership.
- [ ] People describe you as *All work and no play*.
- [ ] You spend little or no money investing in yourself.
- [ ] People think you do not care about yourself.

IMPACT
Risk Factors, Stages & Outcomes

What has already happened or might occur?

- [ ] You learn little about yourself as time goes by.
- [ ] You make the same mistakes over and over.
- [ ] You operate the same way you always have.
- [ ] You feel stressed most of the time.
- [ ] At night, you cannot sleep worrying about things.
- [ ] You have a nervous breakdown.
- [ ] Your abilities and skills do not grow.
- [ ] You fear if you finally slow down, you will have no idea what you would do for yourself.
- [ ] You forget how to relax and have fun.
- [ ] Your body and mind stop functioning.
- [ ] You're tired of or hate what you are doing, and you don't know why.
- [ ] You realize leadership has become your whole life.
- [ ] You realize that your epitaph will be "She worked herself to death."

❏ Your people follow your example and catch the disease.

❏ You are spent and have nothing more to give to your people or those closest to you.

❏ You lose touch with people you have highly valued in the past.

❏ The people who are trying to help you take care of yourself give up.

❏ People quit offering you tickets, trips, perks, or lunch because you always say NO.

❏ You stop evolving and adding value.

★ TREATMENT
Remedy, Prevention & Control

What strategies might work for you? What are you committing to do?

❏ Surround yourself with people who will give you permission to ease up.

❏ When people demand you take time for yourself, do it.

❏ Take time to figure out why you are or have become so resistant to taking time for yourself.

❏ Find a list of personal assessment questions and work through them.

❏ Ask others what they do to take care of themselves.

❏ Make a list of what is truly important to you in your life.

❏ Engage in a creative outlet.

❏ Make a *bucket list* and start working on it.

❏ Balance your time between your mission and your personal development.

❑ Take time for exercise or physical activity.

❑ Keep a journal writing about your feelings and what you are taking from your experiences.

❑ Think through your story: what have you learned; what are your mistakes and successes; what opportunities have been capitalized on or missed?

❑ Schedule time with someone who knows you well so you can share how you feel.

❑ Consider what your life would be like if you had no responsibilities. What would you do?

❑ Take time for meditation or prayer.

❑ Schedule a vacation and take it.

❑ Put on your calendar time for a daily, weekly, or intermittent time for a walk.

❑ Ask people to recommend a good self-help book for thinking and growing.

❑ Put yourself in a position to accept an experience or adventure which will stretch you.

❑ When you hear about a good idea for taking care of yourself, try it.

❑ If you knew you were going to die in one year, what would you change about the way you spend your time?

❑ Go someplace where no one knows you. Do not tell them your titles or credentials.

❑ Ask people you trust to give you feedback on how you could learn and grow.

❑ Schedule a daily nap.

❑ Find a counselor, therapist, or life coach to help you learn about yourself and work on personal improvements.

❑ Find an opportunity to talk to a group about what you learned during your life.

❑ Be intentional with time to recover and rest.

❑ Create a network of leaders who will be a strong resource for you to lean on.

❑ Look in a mirror and tell yourself about all the good you see.

 NOTES
Observations, Reflections & Conclusions

• Has similarities and may overlap with HARMONOPATHY (p. 97).

• UNREFLECTHABITIS (p. 66) is primarily self-imposed and often justified, therefore denying it is an ailment.

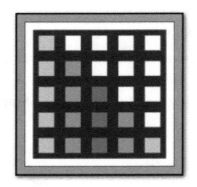

B. CAPACITY

What your load is.
Balance, boundaries, limitations.

Leaders find it difficult to determine their ability to take on more or what is too much. Setting limits for themselves and others is often a struggle. Leaders may be motivated by ambition or success, challenge or service, and commitment, or responsibility. There is a tension between outcome and effort, result and cost, load and capacity, and expectation, and capability. Finding the right balance or load can create conditions which make leaders susceptible to this group of diseases.

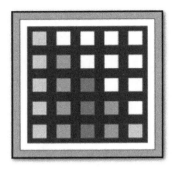

B1. EXPLATONOMY

PRONUNCIATION: eks'-pluh-tahn'-uh-mee

DEFINITION: Overloaded. Too much on your plate. Always taking on more. Inability to say NO. Say YES to everything.

DERIVATION: **EX** = extra + **PLAT**e + **ONO** = on + **MY**

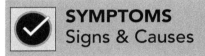

SYMPTOMS
Signs & Causes

Are you experiencing any of these now or in the past? Which apply to you?

❏ You have a continual feeling of being overloaded, overwhelmed, and excessively stressed.

❏ You cannot get to what needs to be done.

❏ When you accept a new responsibility, you strongly feel you can fit it in and get it done.

❏ You wake up at night thinking of all the things that need to be done.

❏ You have a feeling of being over-scheduled.

❏ You are usually quite successful with any leadership role you take on.

❏ You are usually late to scheduled meetings and events.

❏ People remark, "(S)he will never say no."

❏ You want to get things done, you know you can, so you take it on.

❏ You know they really need you in order to succeed

❏ You say YES to please others.

❏ Periodically, you feel like you would like to run away to some remote island and become a hermit.

❏ You enjoy the recognition when stepping into a new leadership position.

❏ You are so overcommitted you cannot get everything done.

❏ You regularly have to choose between multiple obligations within the same time period.

❏ You are regularly worried something is going to fall through the cracks.

❏ People say that you are working too much, and you kind of like their comment.

❏ You think you are spread too thinly.

❏ You take a leadership role because you believe no one else will or can do it as well as you.

❏ Saying YES to leadership roles makes you feel good.

❏ People say, "We can always count on you."

❏ You think your right arm has an automatic upward reflex when someone asks for volunteers.

❏ It feels like your obligations are more than you can handle.

❏ You believe that people admire you for always stepping up.

❏ You are honored to be asked.

❏ You enjoy being a martyr or griping about your load.

❏ You are afraid to say NO because you will lose power or prestige.

❏ When you say, "Let me think about it," but you really don't and say YES anyway.

❏ You feel guilty when you say YES and then do little to nothing.

❏ You are easily excited by new challenges and opportunities.

❏ You feel left out when you are not included.

IMPACT
Risk Factors, Stages & Outcomes

What has already happened or might occur?

❏ People know it will take you a while to get something done.

❏ People are concerned you may or will drop the ball.

❏ Your impact and effectiveness are diminished.

❏ People are resentful because they were counting on you.

❏ Your family and friends get less of your time and attention.

❏ You quit nearly everything or all of your leadership roles.

❏ You feel stressed, trapped, or depressed nearly all the time.

❏ People believe you are always late, and they are usually right.

❏ You burn out because you are worn out.

❏ You cannot find the time to think or consider decisions.

❑ You miss deadlines, scheduled events, and forget more often.

❑ You feel physically ill, and your body does not operate well.

❑ Your reputation is damaged and your impact diminished.

❑ People know they cannot count on your leadership.

❑ Meaningful work is derailed.

❑ You become more tired or more frustrated,

❑ There is a higher probability you may contract Harmonopathy (p. 97).

❑ You cannot and do not get everything done. Things slip through the cracks.

❑ You are easily distracted by competing demands.

❑ People are not sure they can trust you to get things done.

❑ Your relationships with family and friends are damaged.

❑ People quit asking you and you miss some good opportunities.

❑ Your mind is overloaded with tasks, projects, and responsibilities.

★ TREATMENT
Remedy, Prevention & Control

What strategies might work for you? What are you committing to do?

❑ Create criteria for engagement or involvement and use it to decide what you say YES to.

❑ Keep what is most important to you.

❑ Reward yourself for sticking to your NO.

❑ Ask yourself what is worrying you and why?

❑ Make a comprehensive list of your leadership roles or commitments and grade, weigh, and/or valuate them with criteria of your choosing.

❑ State verbally or in writing why you are turning down a request.

❑ Analyze the motivations for why you are involved with each commitment.

❑ Learn about and practice good time management. There are variety of systems and books.

❑ When someone tries to talk you out of NO or into YES, stick with your decision.

❑ Make a list of what is stressing you and focus on handling those items.

❑ Give yourself permission to say NO. And when you say it, be gracious and appreciative.

❑ Wait a while or take some time to think rather than offer a quick YES.

❑ Spend time on tasks which create or leverage more time for you in the future.

❑ Identify things you are most qualified to lead and say NO to what you are not.

❑ Learn what your time cycle is for staying involved with something or when it is time to move on.

❑ Give someone else a chance to learn, grow, and achieve.

❑ Remind yourself that you can have a greater impact when you focus on a few things and do them well.

❑ Determine if you are a *Can't say NO* or *Say YES to everything* person. There is a difference.

❏ Consider if it is a habit or a reflex to say YES. Create a strategy for breaking the pattern.

❏ Create criteria for what is important to you, or what you will say YES to and what gets a NO.

❏ Ask yourself why you are pushing so hard or running at such a fast pace.

❏ Everyone has a rhythm or pace for how you function best. Discover yours.

❏ Get that first NO spoken and see if it makes you feel liberated.

❏ Intentionally schedule time for self, family, and other priorities.

❏ Always ask questions and say "Let me think about it" when you are asked to do something.

NOTES
Observations, Reflections & Conclusions

• Is usually self-inflected.

• May be associated with SUPRAPERFEKTKUS (p. 60) and NDG (NONDELEGATAS) (p. 142).

• May result in contracting HARMONOPATHY (p. 97)

• You may want to look closely at how many of your symptoms relate to pleasing people vs. pleasing self.

• The degree to which you believe something to be important correlates with how quickly you say YES.

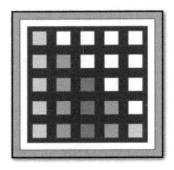

B2. Nomadia

Pronunciation: no-mad'-ee-uh

Definition: Wander around, aimless, lost, confused. Surrender or give up. Not sure where to go or what to do. Unfocused.

Derivation: **NOMAD** = person with no permanent abode who travels from place to place + **IA** = condition or state.

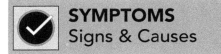

SYMPTOMS
Signs & Causes

Are you experiencing any of these now or in the past? Which apply to you?

❏ You are not sure what to do next week or next month.

❏ You are asking others to give you direction or tell you what you need to do next.

❏ You indulge in self-pity.

❏ You are not taking full responsibility for the efforts you are leading.

❏ You are ignoring or denying your calling.

❏ People say your head is not in the game.

❏ You fear trying something else would be an admission of failing or being ineffective.

❏ You feel you are not worthy of being called a leader.

❏ You no longer pay attention to the essential or the critical details of the organization.

❏ You recognize your path or problem is uncharted, and you have no idea how to approach it.

❏ You are afraid you will fail, so you are frozen.

❏ It feels like you are lost in the desert with hallucinations of being rescued.

❏ You have lost your ambition.

❏ You begin to see that measurable results are deteriorating.

❏ You feel stuck, unable to move.

❏ It seems as though there is no direction to go, or all the choices are bad.

❏ You feel like everything has collapsed and you are at the end.

❏ You used to be overly passionate or extremely committed, but now you feel neither.

❏ You blame yourself for what is happening.

❏ You ask others how to get started.

❏ You feel like a mule with excess baggage (old stuff, not usable) weighing you down.

❏ It seems you or we have tried everything.

❏ You have stopped trying to be the best you can be.

❏ You believe that no one could possibly have a better idea or way than yours.

❑ You have stopped intervening especially when failure appears imminent.

❑ You feel defeated or beaten.

 IMPACT
Risk Factors, Stages & Outcomes

What has already happened or might occur?

❑ Followers begin to slow down and desert your leadership.

❑ People think you look pathetic.

❑ People are concerned and uncertain of what you will say or actions you will take.

❑ People are confused and not sure how to interpret your mixed signals.

❑ Because you are lost, everyone feels lost.

❑ You are labeled a failure.

❑ You lose touch with what is actually going on around you.

❑ People believe you have lost your ability to self-assess and recognize the problem.

❑ You become far removed from the reality of what is truly happening.

❑ People tell you what they think you want to hear.

❑ People feel sorry for you and begin to protect you, making it more difficult to face reality.

❑ People do not give you information because they do not want to surprise or upset you.

❑ You are not in tune with your organization or team.

❏ You feel more pressure on yourself to have all the answers.

❏ You become isolated and you lose contact with the people you need.

❏ Solutions are not sought because everyone believes they are part of a failing effort.

⭐ **TREATMENT**
Remedy, Prevention & Control

What strategies might work for you? What are you committing to do?

❏ Continuously look for avenues of growth for yourself, the organization, or your team.

❏ Calculate a risk, then take it despite the uncertainty awaiting you.

❏ Do something no one would expect.

❏ Trust yourself and your decision making. Recover from your past indecisiveness.

❏ Give yourself permission to ask for help.

❏ Remind yourself that leaders have weaknesses and make mistakes.

❏ Take a break, a hiatus, a sabbatical where you are separated from your leadership role.

❏ Make people aware of growth (no matter how small) assuring them you are improving.

❏ Allow or create a shock therapy approach to force a change or movement.

❏ Adopt some of the treatment strategies in UNREFLECTHABITIS (p. 66).

❏ Allow yourself time to heal or create a time frame for it.

❏ Realize past decisions you made were based on what you knew and understood at the time.

❏ Turn a hopeless situation into hope. Tell people things will be better. Help them believe that.

❏ Establish a rhythm of stress → recover → stress → recover.

❏ Determine what type of activities invigorate you (bring strength to you) and start doing them.

❏ Shift from pessimism to optimism believing the future is bright and you can/will overcome.

❏ Be transparent, admit you have failed or were beaten, let it go, and move on.

❏ Talk to a leader you know who has been through something similar and learn.

❏ Model how recovery and re-investment work.

❏ Proclaim that you are stepping out or aside. Explain why and help people understand.

❏ As a healing process, use your platform to tell your story of how you got here.

❏ Rediscover and restate your goals and motivations.

❏ Engage a mentor, executive coach, or counselor to help you navigate through.

❏ Ask for candid and constructive feedback from your people.

❏ Change your mindset; no one person can have all the answers all the time.

NOTES
Observations, Reflections & Conclusions

- NOMADIA (p. 80) may begin with PODEK (PORDECIPHILIA) (p. 121), or you can experience both at same time.

- How you recover is very important with this disease.

- The nature of this disease can make it difficult for self-recognition.

- If the disease is long term, it may convert into IMPOSTA ATAXIA (p. 92) or NOREFLECTHABITIS (p. 66).

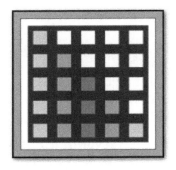

B3. **RSP** (**RELASEATPARESIS**)

PRONUNCIATION: rell a seet' pa ree sis

DEFINITION: Does not know when to step down or aside or release a position. Will not give up seat (at the table). Does not know how to transition roles of leadership.

DERIVATION: **REL** = release + **A** + **SEAT** + **PARESIS** = condition typified by weakness or partial loss of voluntary movement.

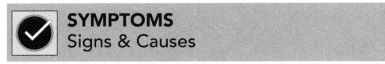

SYMPTOMS
Signs & Causes

Are you experiencing any of these now or in the past? Which apply to you?

❏ You are not sure what you would do if you were not in your leadership role.

❏ You enjoy when people laud your longevity in certain leadership roles.

❏ Some people wonder if they will have to carry your dead body out of your last meeting.

❏ You agree to stay in your leadership role just one more year, again.

❑ At meetings and events, you always have an agenda and targeted people you need to speak to.

❑ You feel like you might lose access to information or your friends if you step down from your role.

❑ You view younger or newer leaders as inexperienced, have not paid their dues, and need to work their way up like you did.

❑ You intentionally or unintentionally leave people out of the information loop.

❑ You are concerned that you will no longer have anything to give back.

❑ You fear that a loss of your role will leave your life empty.

❑ You received your 20-year pin for serving as an officer in an organization.

❑ You do not take the time to introduce aspiring leaders to more establish leaders.

❑ Someone told you that you are clearly one of the *good ole boys (or girls)*.

❑ You are always too busy talking to the important people and have no time for newer folks.

❑ You believe the younger crowd does not understand the issues and problems.

❑ You find yourself standing in a tight circle where no one can catch your eye or gain entry.

❑ It feels like you have been in a specific leadership role forever.

❑ You are concerned you will not know what to do if you step out of your current roles.

❑ You wonder why you are still in certain leadership roles after so many years.

❏ You look around and do not see anyone who aspires to your position.

❏ You are concerned that stepping down might mean you are not valuable and not making a difference.

❏ You think you have served in every position or role in an organization.

❏ You tell yourself you need to stay in the leadership role because no one can or will do it.

❏ You do not want to give up the trappings or perks which come with your role.

 IMPACT
Risk Factors, Stages & Outcomes

What has already happened or might occur?

❏ People view your ideas and approaches as tired, traditional, or not effective.

❏ You are seen as someone who is unwilling to let anyone into the circle, afraid to relinquish power.

❏ People stop seeking your advice.

❏ Younger leaders are resentful of your never-ending engagement.

❏ You are seen as selfish or fearful to step aside.

❏ Your attempt at mentorship is viewed as "Do it my way; it's the only way that works."

❏ A revolt or coup is organized or implemented, and you are the target.

❏ Aspiring leaders are frustrated not seeing a path to ascend in the organization.

❏ Another group creates a different approach and are more effective than what you are doing.

❏ People will not come into your organization because they know you intend on staying forever.

❏ People think you are holding on because you are insecure, or your confidence is waning.

❏ People mutter under their breath, "If I have to hear this story one more time. . . ."

❏ Younger leaders become more vocal and angrier or quiet and withdrawn.

❏ A competing organization or effort is created to challenge your efforts.

❏ You use your leadership influence, capital, and energy to maintain rather than advance the organization you are leading.

TREATMENT
Remedy, Prevention & Control

What strategies might work for you? What are you committing to do?

❏ Know when it is time to lead and when it is time to follow.

❏ Realize that stepping down/aside is an act of courageous leadership.

❏ Ask yourself what you are willing to give up, would be the easiest to release, or should be the first to let go.

❏ Practice the motto of "Leaders create leaders, who create leaders, who create leaders."

❏ Assess what aspects of your life are equal to or greater than your leadership roles.

❏ Instead of being at the table, take a seat in the audience to monitor, observe, reflect, and serve as a resource.

❏ Extol an aspiring leader's attributes when introduced.

❏ Be self-reflective, attuned, and honest with yourself to notice when the leadership shift happens.

❏ Become a mentor or supporter to someone in a new or expanded role of leadership.

❏ Realize leadership does not always mean sitting in the #1 seat (or #2 either).

❏ Find people to replace you telling yourself how important it is for the organization or effort to continue into the future.

❏ Ask others how you can help them in their role.

❏ Rather than you talk, allow or encourage others to tell their stories or their version without interfering.

❏ Take on a role of a convener, collaborator, or facilitator.

❏ Tell yourself that you do not have be in a leadership role to be valuable.

❏ Shift your role to becoming a mentor and advisor whose primary purpose is to listen, support, and encourage.

❏ Take a role of being the institutional memory of the organization to offer perspective, not "We've already done that or that won't work."

❏ Support the ideas of the newer leaders. Offer to help, not takeover.

❏ Move into a role of guidance while listening, suggesting, and affirming.

❏ Search your heart and soul to realize you already know you have stayed too long, need to move on, or take a new role.

NOTES
Observations, Reflections & Conclusions

- Leadership ebbs and flows in communities. The same people are not there forever. They come and go.

- There are other roles of leadership which are important but may not hold a title or be long term.

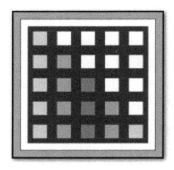

B4. IMPOSTA ATAXIA

PRONUNCIATION: em-pah'-stuh   uh-tack'-see uh

DEFINITION: Your leadership role is beyond your capability. Whether the position was voluntarily engaged or assigned, you do not have the abilities to be successful.

DERIVATION: **IMPOSTA** = imposter + **ATAXIA** = the presence of abnormal, uncoordinated movements.

SYMPTOMS
Signs & Causes

Are you experiencing any of these now or in the past? Which apply to you?

❑ You are or were the obvious or only choice for leader replacement.

❑ You feel like you were not ready for this or got in too soon.

❑ You are miserable and dread it every time you must perform.

❑ You cannot remember why you jumped in or volunteered for this role.

❑ Extol an aspiring leader's attributes when introduced.

❑ You are scared and may not even know why.

❑ You feel unprepared for the position, not sure you possess the abilities needed.

❑ You believe you and your contribution have no value to the organization.

❑ You feel you are past your prime or the right time to serve.

❑ You do not understand the full depth of the responsibility you have taken on.

❑ You discover you were put in the position to fail.

❑ It seems as though people do not trust you.

❑ You cannot see how your role fits into the organization.

❑ You are creating a false sense of power, prestige, or authority to compensate for your shortcomings.

❑ People believe you are pretending to be an expert.

❑ You have feelings of being *in over your head*.

❑ You are making an excessive number of mistakes.

❑ Superiors, colleagues, and others are telling you what to do, and they did not use to do that.

❑ People say, "I guess we need to step in and handle this since our leader (meaning you) is not handling it."

❑ Others are taking over what you believe to be your responsibilities.

❑ They (whoever) are plotting a coup.

❑ You find it difficult to be confident or bold in your actions.

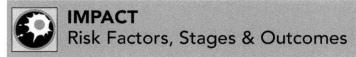

IMPACT
Risk Factors, Stages & Outcomes

What has already happened or might occur?

❏ You fake it, quit, or drown.

❏ Your fear cripples your effectiveness.

❏ Less and less information and resources are available to you, decreasing your effectiveness.

❏ People see through your facade and react in negative ways.

❏ People lose confidence in you and will not follow your leadership.

❏ You suffer in silence and lose confidence.

❏ People avoid involving you in planning and decision making.

❏ People know you are hiding or avoiding your responsibilities.

❏ People view you as ineffective and ignore you.

❏ People talk about you behind your back and are damaging your reputation.

❏ You find a dead critter in your chair letting you know how others feel about your effectiveness.

❏ People are misjudging you, and you are not able to defend yourself.

❏ You fail and are ceremoniously dispatched or publicly humiliated.

❏ Due to your bad experience, a new opportunity appears, and you refuse it (even though you might be ready and capable now).

TREATMENT
Remedy, Prevention & Control

What strategies might work for you? What are you committing to do?

❑ Explore and face your fear.

❑ Seek appropriate training for certification in leadership or required skill areas.

❑ Gain a better understanding of how you got into this position.

❑ Think about why you thought you were prepared or could handle the role.

❑ Ask your team to tell you what you are not doing well. Listen and appreciate.

❑ Admit to others that you are struggling or failing. Ask them to help you.

❑ Seek the advice or engage someone who has been in this or a similar position and was successful.

❑ Obtain an accurate assessment of your strengths and abilities.

❑ Rebuild your confidence by focusing on what you are good at.

❑ Have a recognized or respected source validate what you are doing well.

❑ Leverage the trust, respect, and positive relationships you have with your team.

❑ Leave your leadership position, but assure your replacement is capable of being successful.

❑ Get your team or others invested in your success.

❏ Seek the advice of someone who can help you understand how to step out gracefully.

❏ Realize this position has been a damaging mistake and create a plan on how you recuperate.

❏ Decide that you are going to dedicate yourself to doing whatever it takes make it work.

❏ Be smart enough to know when to get out.

❏ Create an exit strategy.

❏ Go where you can start over or try again.

❏ Cut your losses, quit, or resign.

 NOTES
Observations, Reflections & Conclusions

• Can be self-imposed or self-inflicted.

• External forces or circumstances can place you in this position.

• The disease is often affiliated with NOMADIA (p. 80).

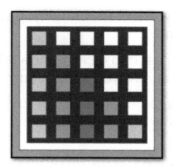

B5. HARMONOPATHY

PRONUNCIATION: har'-Muhn-Ah'-Puh-Thee

DEFINITION: Unable to successfully integrate your personal life with your leadership roles and responsibilities. Difficult in balancing priorities.

DERIVATION: **Harmony** = consistent, orderly, or pleasing arrangement of parts + **OPATHY** = disorder

SYMPTOMS
Signs & Causes

Are you experiencing any of these now or in the past? Which apply to you?

- ❏ You see yourself as a leader in everything you do.
- ❏ Your leadership and personal roles are intertwined.
- ❏ Nearly all of your friends are affiliated with you through your leadership.
- ❏ All of your social media postings involve your leadership roles.
- ❏ You think about events in terms of "I should be there."
- ❏ Your children have forgotten what you look like.

❑ Periodically, you feel as though your priorities are in the wrong place.

❑ You think you used to clearly know what was important in your life, but now you are not sure.

❑ When you attend something for entertainment, your focus is usually on what you have to accomplish for work.

❑ Fairly often, people who are close to you challenge your priorities.

❑ You view relationships as a means to an end.

❑ You approach your relatives as prospects for whatever you are currently trying to promote.

❑ Your spouse/partner complains you are never available for anything outside of your leadership obligations.

❑ It feels like your life is out of control and out of balance.

❑ You think leadership is all about being in the #1 seat.

❑ You panic or are embarrassed when you realize you have forgotten your business cards.

❑ You feel like your leadership is the most important aspect of your life.

❑ Leadership events take precedence over family and friend events.

❑ You now or in the past have had a case of NOREFLECTHABITIS (p. 66).

❑ Someone you value has told you firmly that "Your priorities are really messed up."

❑ A catastrophic event occurred in your life, and it has made you rethink what is truly important to you.

❑ Attending events does not have the same enjoyment as they used to.

❑ People know they can count on you to show up to anything and everything.

❑ You are always dressed to impress or be seen as a professional and not there to play.

❑ You are usually focused on how to get to the next level of leadership.

❑ You realize you are doing things which violate your personal values.

 IMPACT
Risk Factors, Stages & Outcomes

What has already happened or might occur?

❑ Your spouse or partner leaves you.

❑ People believe you will only focus your efforts on what is important for you.

❑ When people want to have fun, they do not invite you because you are all business.

❑ You give up all your leadership roles and walk away from everything.

❑ People feel you do not have time for them or for the friendship you share.

❑ People say this fits you: "All work and no play make Jack a dull boy (or Jill a boring girl)."

❑ You neglect your family and the ones who love you.

❑ You sacrifice your health, accepting fatigue and exhaustion as part of the job.

❑ People avoid you because you always have an agenda.

❑ You stop enjoying and even dread going to events and meetings.

❏ Extol an aspiring leader's attributes when introduced.

❏ Your goals and vision become blurred.

❏ You develop compromising relationships to satisfy your needs for belongingness.

❏ You feel marginalized by family and friends as an unimportant or undependable relationship.

❏ You become depressed, lack energy, and/or lose interest in a personal life.

❏ People stay away from you because you are always selling something, asking for money, or seeking support.

❏ You find personal life, family, and friendships mundane and uninteresting.

❏ What you care about in your leadership roles is in conflict with what you say you care about personally.

★ TREATMENT
Remedy, Prevention & Control

What strategies might work for you? What are you committing to do?

❏ Schedule time for personal reflection.

❏ Determine what other areas of your life are important beyond leadership.

❏ Separate your leadership roles from everyday life.

❏ Refuse to cancel a personal activity so you can fulfill a leadership role.

❏ Determine what a healthy balance looks like for you.

❏ Withdraw from the pressures of leadership and work to maintain perspective.

❏ Use your faith or belief system to guide your decisions on what is important to you and where to invest your time.

❏ Step away from leadership responsibilities and enjoy recreation and relationships.

❏ Reevaluate if what you consider to be a leadership responsibility or obligation is truly that.

❏ Rediscover your sense of *why* things are important to you.

❏ Cancel a leadership activity to spend time with your spouse, a family member, or friend.

❏ Take time to reaffirm or clarify your vision and goals.

❏ Imagine how the organization could successfully function without you.

❏ Recharge your spiritual batteries.

❏ Carve out an hour every day, part of a day every week, or a full day monthly for maintaining your creativity and perspective in pursuit of your goals.

❏ Balance the demands of your time by properly prioritizing your leadership obligations with family and friend relationships, mental and physical health, and time for reflection and personal growth.

❏ Consider how technology can enhance your balance rather than keep it imbalanced.

❏ Spend time with someone you trust and ask that person for recommendations on how you can get your life in better balance.

❏ Talk to someone who seems to have their leadership and personal life in a healthy balance.

❏ Schedule regular activities (weekly, monthly, yearly) with your spouse, family, or friends.

❑ Develop relationships outside your *comfort zone* and with people who have different perspectives about life.

NOTES
Observations, Reflections & Conclusions

- The focus of this disease is confused or misplaced priorities and how your role allows you to leverage being a more effective leader.

- Most leaders seem to acknowledge that HARMONOPATHY (p. 97) exists with other leaders but have a difficult time recognizing it in themselves.

- It is difficult for many leaders to separate or understand the distinction between real friends and those relationships which create opportunity or impose barriers.

- This can become a companion disease when infected by EXPLATONOMY (p. 74) and NOREFLECTHABITIS (p. 66).

C. STYLE

How you handle your role. Methods, philosophy.

Style refers to a leader's characteristic behaviors when directing, motivating, guiding, and managing people. Leaders can also motivate others to perform, create, and innovate. There are often vast differences in how people lead. Theories and frameworks allow us to better identify and understand different leadership styles.

C1. Duorditis

Pronunciation: doo'-ohr-dai'-tuhs

Definition: You or your people will get it done no matter what it takes or cost.

Derivation: **DU** = do + **OR** = or + **D** = die + **ITIS** = inflamation

 SYMPTOMS
Signs & Causes

Are you experiencing any of these now or in the past? Which apply to you?

❏ You are constantly saying, "Let's hurry up, get this done."

❏ You have always taken the approach of it's all in or nothing.

❏ You believe winners never give up or walk away (even for a moment).

❏ You hear your people say, "If we keep up this pace, we are all gonna die."

❏ You do not consider yourself to be a planner or good strategist.

❑ People push back when you push hard.

❑ You think if you lose people due to exhaustion or inability, you can replace them.

❑ You believe failure is not an option. It will not happen to you.

❑ You are convinced you must reach your goal.

❑ Planning and preparation are often in short supply.

❑ You believe all good things come to those who work hard or get the job done.

❑ You hear people say, "I didn't sign up for this."

❑ You think it is a waste of time to talk it over or think it through before you start.

❑ You believe the nature of what you are doing demands great sacrifice.

❑ The plan is usually in your head, and no one or few others know about it.

❑ Your organization has high turnover.

❑ You know the approach "Keep at it, whatever it takes" has never failed you.

❑ You are afraid of what will happen if you walk away or change course.

❑ You do not like to consider consequences or repercussions.

❑ Often, there is no planning phase, feasibility study, or discussion before a project starts.

❑ You tend to prioritize work over all else.

❑ People often quit because they are burned out.

❑ People in your organization believe and think some or all of the statements above about you.

IMPACT
Risk Factors, Stages & Outcomes

What has already happened or might occur?

❑ People don't see the reason for killing themselves on a project, so they reduce their efforts.

❑ People feel they are or will become collateral damage.

❑ You are blind to mistakes/inefficiencies, and they are damaging you and your people.

❑ Your people are exhausted, and their performance drops dramatically.

❑ Your fears overwhelm you, and you make decisions because you are afraid to fail.

❑ People do not understand how they will benefit from this level of effort and sacrifice.

❑ You lose your best people.

❑ You focus on efficiency and quality suffers.

❑ You make quick decisions or make mistakes that build on each other.

❑ People don't want to be part of what you are doing because you care about getting it done, not them.

❑ You end up not listening or just hearing what you want to hear.

❑ You make projects bigger than they need to be.

❑ Your people begin to rebel by (you fill in the method).

❑ Your people bail because they do not want to be part of the cost.

❑ It did not get done or it failed, and now you must count the cost.

❏ No one wants to work for you because you are a known *slave driver*.

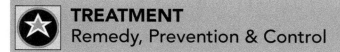

TREATMENT
Remedy, Prevention & Control

What strategies might work for you? What are you committing to do?

❏ Ask yourself why you feel compelled do it no matter the cost.

❏ Consider what the cost may be at its worse, then ask yourself if you are willing to pay that price.

❏ Engage your people in the decision to take on a highly difficult challenge or make a major commitment.

❏ Decide to reduce your efforts (for long or short run) and announce that it is because you care about your people and the price they are paying.

❏ Ask yourself, "Are the outcomes really about me, my values, or sense of worth?"

❏ Stop, take a breath, and examine how you feel. If you have peace in your spirit, proceed.

❏ Announce in advance and provide rewards for those who are sacrificing.

❏ Ask people to make a choice of whether they want to do it at high cost or not.

❏ Ask your people what they see as the outcomes of a maximum effort.

❏ Break your effort into segments. Set times to pause, evaluate, and make a *go-or-no-go* decision.

❏ Consider what is keeping you from changing course or stopping.

❏ Engage your people in creating a plan, conducting a feasibility study, or discussing the parameters before you commit.

❏ Be aware of and even acknowledge the sacrifices your team is making. Don't just expect them.

 NOTES
Observations, Reflections & Conclusions

• This disease foments in environments where time sensitive issues and pressure exist.

• Pressure and urgency are often created by the leader, making the DUORDITIS (p. 106) self-inflicted.

• Leaders with high demands and expectations can cause other leaders to become infected.

• There is a strong correlation of this disease with HARMONOPATHY (p. 97).

• There are times when the aspects of DUORDITIS (p. 106) are used as a strategy when there is need for an emergency response or the outcomes are too important to abandon.

C2. RAPISTRUKITIS

PRONUNCIATION: rap'-ih-struh-kai'-tis

DEFINITION: Rushing to create structure, form, or process. Utilizes a traditional or common approach with the same people.

DERIVATION: **RAPI** = rapid + **STRUK** = structure + **ITIS** = inflammation

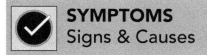

SYMPTOMS
Signs & Causes

Are you experiencing any of these now or in the past? Which apply to you?

❏ You love to plan and put together what is needed to get your project going.

❏ You usually know what needs to be done, so you organize it.

❏ Not being sure what else to do, you create structure and/or process.

❏ You think creating and utilizing surveys are really important, if not essential.

❑ You know there are always going to be people who are disgruntled with what is being done.

❑ You ignore the *why* and quickly move to the *what* and *how*.

❑ You spend a tremendous amount of your time in planning.

❑ You have heard that people do not trust what will happen in your meeting.

❑ You believe it is important to create structure before taking any action.

❑ Most of the time, you have what needs to be done all thought out in your head.

❑ You believe nearly every problem can be handled by convening a group of people to address it.

❑ You believe that no project should begin without a well thought out plan with lots of detail.

❑ Someone says, "We need to . . . ", and you jump in saying, "I can put a plan together to make that happen."

❑ You believe that spontaneity and immediate action usually lead to poor results.

❑ You are addicted to Survey Monkey or similar tools.

❑ You believe that organization is the key to success.

❑ You rush to organize because you know what needs to be done and you are good at making it happen.

❑ You get quite irritated with people who complain they were left out of the planning or process.

❑ You think rules, policies, procedures, and guidelines are all very important.

❑ You believe that every effort should start with research like questionnaires, focus groups, and interviews.

❏ People view you as one of the people always in charge.

❏ You are seen by others as always taking the same approach.

❏ You usually use the same people to do the planning.

❏ People complain about lack of transparency, and you feel your group was absolutely transparent.

❏ You do not understand why some people think there are too many rules and procedures.

 IMPACT
Risk Factors, Stages & Outcomes

What has already happened or might occur?

❏ Others do not trust you because you always seem to be making the rules.

❏ People feel left out because they are always outside the process.

❏ People are not sure what the plan is, how it was put together, or how it will be done.

❏ People believe they will never get picked to serve or be in what they call *on the inside.*

❏ People are angry or frustrated because it's always the same people putting things together.

❏ People attempt to sabotage or derail your efforts.

❏ People rebel against *more* meetings, government, taxes, dues, rules, and other detail.

❏ People know you are always one of the people who make the rules.

❏ People become loudly vocal because they feel unheard or outnumbered.

❏ A strong *we against them* atmosphere dominates.

❏ People believe that information is being hidden from them.

❏ Trust becomes very difficult or nearly impossible to build.

❏ You spend a tremendous amount of time trying to deal with those who are disgruntled and distrustful.

❏ People feel like you and a few others make the plans, and then they have to implement them.

★ TREATMENT
Remedy, Prevention & Control

What strategies might work for you? What are you committing to do?

❏ Have an in-depth discussion as to *why* you feel a problem or issue needs attention.

❏ Ask yourself what you are trying to accomplish by creating structures, forms, and processes.

❏ Determine what groups and individuals always feel left out.

❏ Do not mandate, "This is the way we do it."

❏ Meet with and listen to the people who are primarily impacted by your efforts.

❏ Intentionally involve people who are not normally asked.

❏ When you involve new people, take the time to give them an overview and allow them to ask questions.

❏ Do not tell people what the rules are or explain how the game is played without explaining *why* the game is played.

❏ Try a completely different or new approach.

❏ Remember, form follows function, so make sure you know what those functions are.

❏ Do not assume that just because something worked in the past that it will work now.

 NOTES
Observations, Reflections & Conclusions

• Most leaders are good at planning and organizing, so it becomes their default.

• Subtle disease, difficult to detect or leaders do not believe they have contracted it.

• A very complex disease that has residual or recurring long-term detriment.

C3. CRANIALRECTALITIS

PRONUNCIATION: cray-nee-al-rek-ta-lai-tihs

DEFINITION: Cannot see things clearly, obstructed view. Not seeing the real problem(s) or causes. No view of the future.

DERIVATION: **CRANIAL** = relating to the skull or head + RECTAL = relating to the rectum + **ITIS** = inflammation

INTERCHANGEABLE WORDS: challenge, problem, issue, task, project, goal, objective

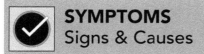

SYMPTOMS
Signs & Causes

Are you experiencing any of these now or in the past? Which apply to you?

❏ More than once, you've heard yourself say, "I didn't see that coming."

❏ You have been accused of not learning from your mistakes.

❏ Your organization or team is filled with people who have similar perspectives and experiences.

❏ People are telling you there is more to the problem, and you argue or ignore them.

❏ You do not value exploration, research, prioritization, or planning for stages and steps.

❏ People have said about you, "He looked like a deer in the headlights."

❏ You have no idea what an environmental scan is.

❏ You seem to regularly have a blind spot when it comes to certain issues.

❏ You usually believe you have plenty of information to move forward. You do not need any more.

❏ It seems like there are always major issues popping up.

❏ You spend little to no time talking with your competitors or allies.

❏ People tell stories (and chuckle) about your poor handling of a situation when you did not have all the facts.

❏ You have never done a stakeholder analysis.

❏ There are times when people repeatedly tell you the problem is unresolved.

❏ You have experiences of fixing something, and it does not get better, just worse.

❏ You have not taken the time to think into the future and consider what it looks like for your organization or field.

❏ A phrase which comes into your mind often is: "I must have had my head up my ass."

❏ You often feel like you were completely caught off guard.

❏ You seldom seek to involve a diverse group of people to evaluate a problem or issue.

❏ You hear yourself often saying "Well, that's what happens when you assume."

IMPACT
Risk Factors, Stages & Outcomes

What has already happened or might occur?

- ❏ Addressing barriers and problems is not integrated into goals or tasks.

- ❏ Poor decisions are made based upon incomplete data.

- ❏ People believe you are not very smart because you do not have a clear view and understanding of a challenge.

- ❏ There are always additional issues or more complex consequences you hadn't considered.

- ❏ Others talk about stories of how you poorly handled a situation without all the facts.

- ❏ You proceed without having all the information you need.

- ❏ People see you caught off guard so often, they think is OK when it happens to them.

- ❏ Problems and issues continue to come from nowhere.

- ❏ It becomes part of your culture to be unprepared and caught off guard.

- ❏ You and your organization spend extra time and money to get it right.

- ❏ You look at the symptoms, results, and impact rather than causal factors.

- ❏ Your competitors and enemies take advantage of your blunders.

- ❏ You routinely do not conduct any types of analyses.

- ❏ People are afraid to tell you the problem is unresolved because they do not want to argue with you.

- ❏ You and your people spend an excessive amount of time putting out fires.

❑ People will not share information with you because they believe you will ignore it anyway.

❑ People want to see you fail to prove you are the idiot they believe you to be.

❑ You and your people will continue to not review failures or learn from them.

❑ Your exposure to what is going on around you continues to constrict.

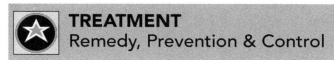

TREATMENT
Remedy, Prevention & Control

What strategies might work for you? What are you committing to do?

❑ Ask yourself: What would make this project fail? What is required to make it successful?

❑ Find and utilize people who have the disease of RAPISTRUKITIS (p. 111), since they love analysis, research, and planning.

❑ Encourage people to come to you early and often with problems.

❑ Read and explore other fields, sectors, industries, and arenas about which you know nothing.

❑ Construct a comprehensive list of all the possible outcomes, good and bad.

❑ Physically stand or sit in different space when discussing or analyzing a problem.

❑ Invite people with different perspectives to discuss an issue.

❑ Create a list of assumptions you are making about a problem or situation.

❏ Listen to or read the thoughts and projections of futurists.

❏ Learn how to surveille or scan a situation before you jump in.

❏ Assign people to be your *eyes and ears* and to come back and report.

❏ Find smart people in a completely different field, pose a problem to them, and listen to their thoughts.

❏ Give people permission to challenge you with "I think you (we) are missing some things."

❏ Reward people for bringing unnoticed issues to your attention.

❏ Stop simply doing and take the time to observe and listen.

 NOTES
Observations, Reflections & Conclusions

• Strong correlation with PODEK (p. 121).

• A leader is always facing problems and issues. A high level of awareness is very important.

• Consider the distinctions of sightless vs. confused. One is without opening for admitting lights or seeing through, and the other refers to being not directed or controlled by reason. Both could involve acting without seeing and investigating first.

C4. **PODEK** (Pordeciphilia)

Pronunciation: por'-duh-see-fih'-lee-uh

Definition: Poor decision making, inability to decide.

Derivation: **POoR** + **DECI**sion + **PHILIA** = attraction to or tendency

SYMPTOMS
Signs & Causes

Are you experiencing any of these now or in the past? Which apply to you?

❏ You think if I can just solve this problem, everything will be better.

❏ You frequently think you have the answer, and it is so simple.

❏ You know in your heart you do not truly or fully understand, but you want to get moving or resolve it, or you are being pressured to.

❏ You often tell yourself that you are over thinking, over analyzing, or over complicating it.

❏ You know the right thing is more difficult to do, so you select the easier way.

❏ You are overwhelmed by a big problem, so you avoid its complexity.

❏ When there are problems, you classify them as no big deal, just a passing phase, a bump in the road, or a blip on the radar screen.

❏ You cannot or will not make the hard decisions.

❏ You second guess or rethink most of your decisions.

❏ Your tender heart hampers your ability to address serious problems with people.

❏ You fear or have had bad experiences with analysis paralysis.

❏ You ignore data because you usually know what is best, and your assumptions have been good.

❏ You ignore the process of collect data, make assumptions, then decide. Instead, you rush to either the assumption or *just decide* stage.

❏ You *jump the gun* before you or the team have all the information you need.

❏ You delay your decisions as long as you can.

❏ You are quick to react, and you see this as a good trait in yourself.

❏ You do not like to get too many people involved. It only confuses things.

❏ You fear you will make the wrong decision.

❏ When someone says, "That was a bad decision," you ignore the comment or excuse it.

❏ You are often caught making assumptions which lead to poor outcomes.

❏ You fail to tell people about the process you used or the decision you have made.

❏ You do not believe measurable results are important.

- When things go wrong, you feel vindicated because you did not decide.
- You think you have adequate information, and you discover you do not.
- You have a difficult time distinguishing between urgent vs. not urgent, and important vs. not important.

IMPACT
Risk Factors, Stages & Outcomes

What has already happened or might occur?

- You overlook factors which are critical.
- You are not aware of the flaws in your process for making decisions.
- Your solution fixes in the short term but has little or no long-term impact.
- The problem or issue continues because your approach was not effective.
- People question or reduce their efforts to research, gather data, and collect information since it is either ignored or given little relevance.
- People feel they have little value since you do not consider their input, and you make your decisions anyway.
- You or your team fail to identify the root cause of the problem.
- Intended and unintended consequences are not given enough review.
- You do not recognize bad decisions.
- Others lose respect for you as the leader.
- Opportunities are missed, some of which are critical.
- Because the real problem is not contained, a domino effect is created.

❑ Emotions are allowed to over-interfere in your decisions.

❑ You gain a reputation for being a procrastinator.

❑ Ultimately morale is driven to its knees.

❑ Not enough time is taken to analyze when the solution did not fix the problem.

❑ You tolerate situations which could obviously be corrected.

❑ Teamwork environment is severely.

❑ People are discouraged from finding a better solution.

❑ Lots of wasted time which cost *moola*!!

❑ People think you are not doing your job.

❑ Fear of failure, loss of status, loss of power, and/or loss of position cripple you.

❑ You allow the unimportant and non-urgent task to consume your time taking you away from decisions.

❑ You are be perceived as negative because inaction has a negative effect.

❑ Emergencies become dangerous.

❑ Everyone is frustrated.

❑ Stakeholders will lose trust, and everyone will suffer due to your indecision.

❑ People see you as not having the will to do what is right or most important.

❑ Your mind is cluttered by too many issues.

★ TREATMENT
Remedy, Prevention & Control

What strategies might work for you? What are you committing to do?

❑ Ask WHY? 100 times.

❑ If it seems easy, remind yourself and others that it is probably not.

❑ Rather than think problems are simple and have simple solutions, consider that they are more complex than you imagine.

❑ Rather than spending time wrestling with what to do, select a more thorough approach and get going.

❑ Recognize each problem has the potential to be unique and calls for situational leadership.

❑ Ask and allow mid-level leaders to make decisions.

❑ Realize the process may be more valuable than reaching an end result or outcome.

❑ Ask clarifying questions to get the most truth possible before you or we arrive at a decision.

❑ Integrate faith, meditation, or spirituality into your process.

❑ Break the process into several smaller decisions which create a more limited set of actions.

❑ Have a retreat with your leadership team to analyze the decision-making process in your organization.

❑ Ask yourself if you are focused on the right things.

❑ Ask your people what decision needs to be made, by whom, and when.

❑ Clarify who is responsible for which decisions.

❑ Hold people and teams accountable for their decisions.

❑ Allow an extra day or two to consider your decision.

❑ Identify clear alternatives to determine which may be best and worse.

❑ You do not recognize bad decisions.

❑ Take time to weigh the available evidence and allocate adequate time to implement.

❏ Others lose respect for you as the leader.

❏ Set a time and an agenda to review recent or past decisions and their consequences.

❏ Take yourself out of the equation where you make all the decisions.

❏ Define the process for shared decision making and implement it.

❏ If it is a tossup whether to take a simple or complex approach, select the complex because you know you will gain more from it.

❏ Evaluate circumstances to allow for well measured and decisive decision making.

❏ Consider if your passion is clouding your judgment.

❏ Take no action and let your decision sit 24 hours before implementation. In other words, sleep on it.

 NOTES
Observations, Reflections & Conclusions

• There is often a tension in decision making between too fast vs. too slow, too thorough vs. not thorough enough.

• Some leaders tend to take the simple or rushed approach due to their desire to get things done quickly.

• It's not always bad decisions, sometimes there are just bad choices.

• Some of the impacts of this PODEK (PORDCIPHILIA) (p. 121) are similar to CRANIALRECTALITIS (p. 116).

C5. OPTOPENIA

PRONUNCIATION: ahp'-tuh-pee'-nee-uh

DEFINITION: inability to convey vision or expectations, not visionary enough. Cannot get buy in.

DERIVATION: **OPTO** = denoting vision + **PENIA** = deficiency

INTERCHANGEABLE WORDS: Group A: vision, expectations, mission, goals, direction, purpose, objectives, strategy. Group B: unknown, unclear, undecided, unsettled, unproven, indeterminate, doubtful, equivocal, faint, irresolute, obscure, pending, vague, wavering, abeyant.

SYMPTOMS
Signs & Causes

Are you experiencing any of these now or in the past? Which apply to you?

- ❏ You spend a significant amount of time talking about the unknown or the past.

- ❏ It seems like you can see something (vision), but others cannot.

- ❏ You have a difficult time explaining your vision for the organization.

❏ People do not understand the direction you are going.

❏ Few can recite your vision or mission statements (or even parts of them).

❏ People cannot explain the purpose of what they are doing, or worse, it makes no sense to them.

❏ You do not know how to differentiate between why it is important and that it needs to be done.

❏ You get frustrated because people usually fall short of your expectations.

❏ You get very upset when people challenge your direction.

❏ The mission of your organization is just words on a wall, and people don't know where the wall is.

❏ You are not sure where you are headed and are confused by it.

❏ You become frustrated, disappointed, or even angry because people don't get it.

❏ When you talk about the direction and vision, people look like they have dead eyes.

❏ You and your people spend excessive amounts of time arguing about the differences between mission and vision, goals, and objectives, etc.

❏ When your people are asked to recite a purpose statement, most silently move their lips.

❏ There is no orientation or on-boarding process for new people to learn the strategies.

❏ You usually provide your ideas and solutions before allowing others to share theirs.

❏ You complain and commiserate with other leaders (inside and outside) on why your people seem so lost.

❏ It seems like people get really fired up when you talk about the future, and then their enthusiasm drops.

❏ You tell the same stories over and over or in the same way because you don't think people understand them.

❏ Others think it is OK to not focus on the mission because you do not.

❏ You think the mission of the organization is not right and your mission is better suited.

❏ It seems people generally have no buy-in to the direction you are headed.

❏ You like to argue about definitions of planning terminology, models, and concepts.

❏ You have a good idea of where you want to go but are unsure of how to get there.

❏ You want your people to agree with what you are doing and the direction you are taking.

IMPACT
Risk Factors, Stages & Outcomes

What has already happened or might occur?

❏ Customers and members are not confident in your efforts.

❏ Enthusiasm and commitment diminish over time.

❏ People wander around aimlessly wasting time since they are not clear on the direction.

❏ In the absence of a clear vision or unified goals, people create their own.

❏ People create competing directions and sometimes isolate you from discovering them.

❑ Conflicts are created due to no agreed-upon strategy.

❑ You assume people are with you, but they are not.

❑ Others believe you have all the answers in your head, but they are not sure what to do.

❑ Some people are just turned off by the confusion or lack of clarity.

❑ People will not propose objectives, projects, or tasks because they don't know how they fit.

❑ It's apparent that you have it all thought out, but people don't want to follow you blindly.

❑ People think you do not trust them because the direction seems to be secret.

❑ People ask, what they can do, look puzzled, or keep asking more questions.

❑ You interpret lack of questions or false smiles as support.

❑ People will say "It's a good idea," when they really don't believe it is.

❑ People wonder if there is a hidden agenda.

❑ People like you and want you to be successful, but they have no idea where you are going.

❑ Your explanations appear to others as if you trying to prove you are right.

❑ People are confused.

❑ You change the direction of the organization and people do not like it.

❑ You focus on what makes you look good.

❑ Your needs and wants to become more important than the mission.

- ❏ Decisions are based on different criteria than the mission.
- ❏ Organizational members are frustrated.
- ❏ People work aimlessly with no direction.
- ❏ People are not focused on guiding principles and strategies.
- ❏ You get lost between the vision for the organization and what will benefit you.
- ❏ People think you ARE the vision, not the goals or mission of the organization.
- ❏ You assume everyone is with you, then you are surprised when they don't follow through or worse.

★ TREATMENT
Remedy, Prevention & Control

What strategies might work for you? What are you committing to do?

- ❏ Talk about where you (we) are going, what we are going to do, and what the future looks like.
- ❏ Spend 50% of your time communicating the vision/ mission/ strategy to your people.
- ❏ Compliment actions that support the mission and explain why.
- ❏ Reward those who exemplify pursuit of the vision.
- ❏ Tell stories and share analogies that have meaning and explain the direction.
- ❏ Assess if you and your people have measurable results or attainable goals. If not, establish them.
- ❏ Create a functional process for creating and implementing a strategic plan.

❑ If you and your team believe it's right, trust the process which has been created or is in place.

❑ Help people understand how risk and reward are part of the direction.

❑ Assess if your mission or strategic direction is still relevant or timely.

❑ Tell people stories which convey important principles or values.

❑ Change your culture to be mission focused.

❑ Reinforce the belief that *mission is the key to all we do.*

❑ Help people discover what aspects of their experiences connect to organization's mission.

❑ Establish a weekly (or regular) meeting to talk about only direction, mission, vision, future.

❑ Keep a focus on the mission by aligning your actions with it.

❑ Assure people that decisions are made and being made based on the mission.

❑ Handle your leadership role as if it is the last mission, you will ever undertake.

❑ Include people in constructing and revising the strategic direction of the organization.

❑ Help people feel the enthusiasm, passion, or commitment to the mission.

❑ Help people understand how the mission aligns with what's in it for them.

❑ Assess how credible you are for people to believe you know where you are headed.

❑ Celebrate successes along the way.

❑ Assess the level of buy-in you have at the top and bottom of the organization.

❏ Encourage questioning and be open to diverse views.

❏ Determine how inspiring or motivational your vision is.

❏ Make sure your mission is the right one for the right time. Assure it's on target.

❏ Lead your team to common goals using a mutually developed strategy.

❏ Schedule regular performance reviews with all team members to assure they understand your expectations and are performing.

NOTES
Observations, Reflections & Conclusions

• Team members are not the only ones who are impacted by this OPTOPENIA (p. 127). So are stakeholders.

C6. COMPASSLESS

PRONUNCIATION: kuhm'-puhs-less

DEFINITION: Unable to understand or navigate change.

DERIVATION: **COMPASS** = instrument which shows direction + **LESS** = absent or missing

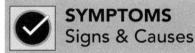

SYMPTOMS
Signs & Causes

Are you experiencing any of these now or in the past? Which apply to you?

❏ You do not like change.

❏ When people present a change, your default is to resist it.

❏ You believe when everything is going well, do not make changes.

❏ People who propose to do things differently are irritating.

❏ You like to be with people who like the status quo.

❏ There has never been a dramatic change in your life.

❏ You love telling stories about the way it used to be or *the good ole days*.

❏ You wait until you are forced to change, and then you react.

❑ You believe you and your people are highly unlikely to face a crisis.

❑ You often hear the phrase, "What in the hell is going on?"

❑ When there is a change, you think it is best to just roll with it.

❑ You fear that change is going to destroy you or your efforts.

❑ You adhere to the motto, "We have been doing it this way forever and it has always worked."

❑ You believe crisis planning is a waste of time and resources.

❑ You believe if something dramatic occurs, you can handle it.

❑ Change makes you nervous about the potential outcomes.

❑ You hate to talk about change because it seems to create great negativity and fear.

❑ You have seen many others change and fail.

❑ You hear your people saying, "Everything is going crazy out there" or something similar.

❑ You believe if you wait long enough, everything will return to normal or will turn out OK.

IMPACT
Risk Factors, Stages & Outcomes

What has already happened or might occur?

❑ You inadvertently create a culture of fear and resistance to change.

❑ People develop dysfunctional ways to cope with change.

❑ You become blind to recognizing when change is happening.

❏ Your people realize you will not address necessary or needed change.

❏ People think you are lost and do not know what to do during a major change.

❏ Your people are afraid of change.

❏ You have difficultly balancing time effectively during a crisis.

❏ People see change is happening all around and cannot figure out why you don't.

❏ Your organization and your endeavors begin to collapse or die.

❏ Your competitors move ahead, and you fall behind.

❏ Your people see others responding well to change, and fear your organization is regressing.

❏ People leave because they believe your organization is not handling change well.

❏ People feel change challenges or questions their values.

❏ People view your efforts as stagnant and *old school*.

❏ People fight or resist change.

❏ People speculate on how the change is going to directly impact them.

❏ People leave because they like or thrive on change.

⭐ TREATMENT
Remedy, Prevention & Control

What strategies might work for you? What are you committing to do?

❏ Ask your people what scares them during change.

❏ Respond to their fears.

❏ Recognize that a crisis likely requires a change and must be addressed.

❏ Understand the concept of *embracing change* and what it means to navigate through it.

❏ Analyze how impending change will impact your operations.

❏ Read and study about change and how to manage it.

❏ Visibly display (for you and/or others) a positive motto about change.

❏ Create a timetable for a change and assure everyone understands it.

❏ Explain why, where, when, and how the change is coming.

❏ Differentiate between needing a change and reacting to a mistake.

❏ Make sure outcomes are understandable and meaningful to your people.

❏ Challenge and rethink all your assumptions. Guide that process for your people.

❏ Tie your outcomes to a new direction.

❏ Reinvent your vision, mission, purpose, or direction.

❏ Conduct an environmental scan.

❏ Change from a static thinker to a dynamic one.

❏ Ask others to suggest books or articles on change, change management, and/or change strategies.

❏ Educate your people on what change is and how it can positively or negatively impact outcomes.

❏ Identify and offer praise when aspects of a change are being handled well, by whom, and how.

❏ Seek help from someone who is great at handling change.

❏ Glean the lessons learned on the journey.

❏ Analyze your VUCA world, asking what is volatile, uncertain, complex, and ambiguous.

❏ Study stories of people who have handled change well or triumphed from it.

 NOTES
Observations, Reflections & Conclusions

• We are in a world where change is continuous, fast, and dramatic.

• Change can build character or tear it down.

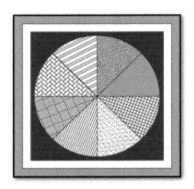

D. ASSIGNMENT

Who does the work.
Allocation, designation,
responsibility.

Leaders assign and delegate responsibilities and authority. They designate roles, assign duties, allocate resources, apportion projects, and track efforts. As assignments are dispersed,

myriad reactions and behaviors ensue. The decisions and methods used by the leader can create dynamics which are a breeding ground for leadership diseases.

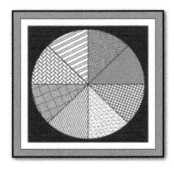

D1. NDG (Nodelegatus)

Pronunciation: noh'-dehl-uh-gay'-tuhs

Definition: Inability to delegate, can do it all. Cannot or will not assign tasks, projects, or responsibilities to others.

Derivation: **NO** + **DELEGA**te + **TUS** = to us

SYMPTOMS
Signs & Causes

Are you experiencing any of these now or in the past? Which apply to you?

❏ You can do it better and faster than anyone else.

❏ No one can present or sell your organization or your efforts better than you.

❏ You cannot count on people to get things done.

❏ Many or most of your people are useless or have little to offer.

❏ You believe a great method of delegation is to hand off identical tasks to two or more people and see who does the best.

❏ You do not allow people to handle money issues, financial matters, or what you call *your money.*

❑ It's challenging for you to clearly explain an assignment or what you expect.

❑ It's just easier to do it yourself.

❑ You wonder why you seem to give the wrong assignments to the wrong people.

❑ You are good at creating new ideas; therefore, you know it will be better.

❑ Since you know the most, you should automatically be the one to lead or be most involved.

❑ Your method of drawing a name and a task from buckets, then matching them, does not work.

❑ It is very upsetting when people tell you they have not completed their assignments.

❑ You do not like to monitor or track what and how people are doing.

❑ You want or deserve all the credit because you did most of the work.

❑ You do not trust that your people can do it or do it to the level you expect.

❑ It is difficult for you to trust other people.

❑ It's done right and timely when you do it.

❑ You are not sure how to delegate whether as responsibilities, projects, goals, or tasks.

❑ It seems people often let you down.

❑ It seems as though you have pretty good control over what is going on.

❑ You believe that no one can work as hard as you.

❑ It is difficult for you to break projects into tasks and steps.

❑ You feel drained of energy due to the weight of your decisions, workload, and responsibilities.

❑ It seems as though you are always the leader on any project.

❑ Since your people seem confused or do not understand, it is better to do it yourself.

❑ Because of your close relationships, you feel that putting more work on others will add to their suffering, so you do it yourself.

 IMPACT
Risk Factors, Stages & Outcomes

What has already happened or might occur?

❑ People do not get a clear signal to proceed.

❑ People do not understand expectations.

❑ You get frustrated and angry because no one else is carrying the load or helping.

❑ You feel like you are the only one really working, producing, or accomplishing.

❑ After you have worn out, you burn out.

❑ People learn to wait for your instructions or be told what to do.

❑ People are unproductive because they have little or nothing to do.

❑ People question their abilities because you never give them difficult assignments.

❑ People have a difficult time operating when you are not there.

❑ People fail to share ideas.

❑ You do not follow up on what is assigned; therefore, it is interpreted as not important.

❑ Some people feel robbed of true growth opportunities.

❑ People do not take ownership of their work or pride in their job.

❑ You do not understand the importance of something; therefore, you do not assign it.

❑ In order to assure completion, double assignments are made which create conflicts.

❑ People feel you do not trust them; therefore, they do not trust you.

❑ People are frustrated or feel alienated at not being given responsibilities.

❑ Your people have no enthusiasm for implementation.

❑ People note that you only check on what you care about; therefore, the rest must be unimportant.

❑ You have robots for workers or that type is attracted to following you.

❑ Your highly motivated people get tired of having little responsibility or few tasks to do.

❑ People work around you, and do not tell you what they are doing.

❑ There is conscious or subconscious subversion by your people. They would like to see you fail.

❑ People do not experience satisfaction or fulfillment in their work.

 TREATMENT
Remedy, Prevention & Control

What strategies might work for you? What are you committing to do?

❑ Realize that you cannot do it all, and you will be more effective if others contribute.

❑ Make a list of things you can let go, then delegate.

❑ Stop and try to understand what might be prompting your desire to control.

❑ Remind yourself that leaders create leaders who create leaders who create leaders.

❑ Assess skills and delegate to people's strengths and interests. Listen to what they think they can do.

❑ Put fear of failure aside and trust subordinates to handle the work.

❑ Take the time you would spend on the task and train someone. In the long run, it will save you both time and effort.

❑ You do not have to hand everything over at once. Take baby steps.

❑ Break assignments or projects into pieces, stages, or levels. Give out these responsibilities a few at a time and see how they do.

❑ Praise others who complete tasks well or better than you.

❑ Be careful to not gladly hand off only the easier or menial tasks.

❑ Tell people you are sure they have the ability, and you know they will get it done.

❑ Tell yourself, this is not easy for me, but I am going to change because (make your list of reasons).

❑ Create an environment or culture where people feel satisfaction and pride.

❑ Ask people what you could do to be a better delegator.

❑ Create and trust a process of planning and accountability where you release duties and delegate tasks.

❑ Define clear objectives and goals for the organization.

❑ Realize it may take you time to learn to trust, but you must do it and make it happen quickly.

❑ Focus on the ultimate outcome allowing people to use other means to accomplish the objectives.

❑ Build relationships to understand the capabilities of others, where they excel, and what they love to do.

❑ Remind yourself, you were a follower before you were ushered into your role of leadership.

❑ Do not underestimate the abilities of those you do not understand or who are not like you.

❑ Do not always assign menial tasks to people who traditionally get those handed to them (women, people of color, less educated, etc.)

❑ Explain that you want to be a better delegator and need their help.

❑ Consult with people who are good delegators and find out what they do.

❑ Read up on resources on the topic of delegation.

❑ Realize it may take you time to learn to trust, but you must do it and make every effort to make it happen quicker.

❑ Believe that what is delegated will be done. That must be your assumption.

 NOTES
Observations, Reflections & Conclusions

- Highly affects younger or less experienced leaders.
- Strongly related to HYPERMANAGITUS (p. 148).
- Most of the symptoms are built around issues of trust, control, and ego.

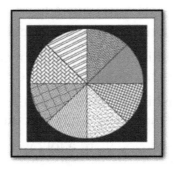

D2. Hypermanagitus

Pronunciation: hai'-pur-man'-uh-jai'-tuhs

Definition: Micromanages everything. Too bossy, tells every-one what to do. Needs to know everything.

Derivation: **HYPER** = obsessive + **MANAG** = manage + **ITIS** = inflammation

SYMPTOMS
Signs & Causes

Are you experiencing any of these now or in the past? Which apply to you?

❏ You often say, "I don't care how you want to do it, do it my way."

❏ Your ideas are always the best.

❏ You want to know 100% of everything going on.

❏ You feel isolated despite being part of everything going on around you.

❏ You tend to select the same people over and over to lead projects.

❏ You notice and critique every detail.

❏ You find yourself often working alone or independently.

❏ You like people who will do exactly what you want and the way you want.

❏ People think you never miss anything.

❏ You have been accused of being a dictator.

❏ You like to keep your fingers in everything.

❏ People complain you are constantly looking over their shoulder.

❏ You over explain instructions to make sure people understand what, why, how, and when.

❏ You are not happy when people do it differently than you want.

❏ You have higher standards than anyone else.

❏ You often find yourself taking over.

❏ You have a certain way you like things done.

❏ You admire leaders who call all the shots.

❏ People just don't understand how to do it the right way.

❏ People seem agitated when you ask a lot of questions.

❏ You have been very successful with your accomplishments.

❏ You like to put your stamp of approval on any decision that is made by someone else.

❏ You want to hear a person's plan before it is executed.

❏ You find yourself in arguments when people try to justify how they did something.

❏ You find it difficult listening to people struggle with how to do something. It is just easier to tell them or do it yourself.

❏ You ask questions, and then answer them yourself.

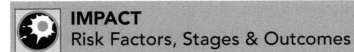

IMPACT
Risk Factors, Stages & Outcomes

What has already happened or might occur?

- ❏ People learn to follow blindly and not ask questions.
- ❏ People are irritated because they do not like the feeling of being controlled.
- ❏ You are disconnected from your people.
- ❏ People quit thinking or adjusting.
- ❏ People feel you do not trust them, or they feel disrespected.
- ❏ People show little initiative while waiting for you to tell them what to do.
- ❏ They reciprocate by not trusting and having respect for you.
- ❏ The culture is defined by pleasing you and those around you.
- ❏ Favoritism creates division as well as a lack of trust.
- ❏ People try to please you rather than create results.
- ❏ People feel you are overcritical.
- ❏ Productivity slows because you are distracting with questions and comments.
- ❏ The creativity and innovation of others are diminished.
- ❏ People are not able to do what they were brought in to do because you are redirecting them.
- ❏ Your team does things the same way they have always been done.
- ❏ While the market or environment changes, people do not adjust but continue to do it the way you want it.

❑ People feel disenfranchised.

❑ Discontentment and worry grow among your people.

❑ The people who have real ability to perform at higher levels leave.

❑ Your people do things behind the scenes and hide it from you.

❑ People tend to feel like they are not valued, and their expertise and skills are not properly utilized.

❑ You experience high turnover with staff, teams, and members.

❑ While trying to manage too much, you pay little attention to areas you do not know much about or feel are unimportant.

❑ People feel they cannot showcase or grow their talents and expertise.

⭐ TREATMENT
Remedy, Prevention & Control

What strategies might work for you? What are you committing to do?

❑ If things are moving along well, step back and let them perform.

❑ When things stop moving forward, regress, or become critical, only then step up and lead.

❑ Create criteria for when it is vital for you to step in, then follow it.

❑ When you feel it is time to step in and take control, ask if your team feels the same way.

❑ Ask people, "How can I help?"

❑ Explain the big picture not all the details.

❏ Recognize people who clearly want to do their job and do it well.

❏ Ask yourself or others if your people were truly listening and understanding.

❏ Deeply explore why you have such a difficult time allowing people to do their job.

❏ When someone volunteers to do something or take a leadership role, allow them to step in.

❏ Ask this question of others: "What would you do in this situation?"

❏ Provide direction, focus, and encouragement, not detailed instructions.

❏ Understand that your role is to cultivate talent.

❏ Reward initiative, innovation, and creativity.

❏ Ask questions to further engage people.

❏ Literally, stop looking over people's shoulders.

❏ Help people understand what success looks like rather than how to achieve it.

❏ Listen to people explain how they are going to do something.

❏ Keep silent until people express their opinions. Count silently to 10 (or higher if needed).

❏ Privately ask why a person performed the way they did.

❏ Let people do what they were brought in to do.

❏ Remember, the HOW is not your job, the WHAT (the goal or outcome being sought) is.

❏ Keep silent knowing that when you open your mouth, you tend to micromanage.

NOTES
Observations, Reflections & Conclusions

- A leader with high standards may be mistaken for HYPERMANAGITUS (p. 148).

- Fear is a strong driver in HYPERMANAGITUS (p. 148). Fear must be faced and may require some therapeutic assistance.

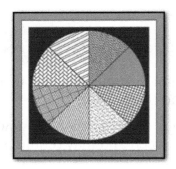

D3. SCLEROSIDRUDGIC

PRONUNCIATION: skleh'-roh-si-druh'-jik

DEFINITION: Are above or too good for routine, mundane, or tedious tasks or those perceived to be of lesser value.

Derivation: **SCLEROSI** = hardening or becoming rigid + **DRUDGIC** = associated with drudgery

INTERCHANGEABLE WORDS: Group A (nouns) task, project, errand, job, assignment, step, duty, chore, charge, function, labor. Group B (adjectives): lousy, low-level, dirty, awful, miserable, boring, unexciting, repetitive, unskilled, humdrum, unwelcome, remedial, uninteresting, simple, useless, second-rate, inferior, vile, worthless, wearisome.

SYMPTOMS
Signs & Causes

Are you experiencing any of these now or in the past? Which apply to you?

❏ You say to others, "You need to do it because, that's how I learned."

❏ Your organization expects new people to get the lousy assignments.

❏ You came up the hard way doing the menial tasks, and that's what it takes to be successful.

❏ You feel important people should not have to do mundane tasks, and you are important.

❏ One of your favorite sayings is, "Everyone knows s*** flows downhill."

❏ You became successful so you could have someone run your errands.

❏ It would make you look bad if someone saw you doing such low-level duties.

❏ You don't like to do unskilled kinds of labor.

❏ You are the boss (leader), and you don't have to do the lousy jobs.

❏ You promised yourself when you made enough money, you would never clean the office restroom again.

❏ You like to occasionally demonstrate that you are not above a low-level task, so you make sure everyone sees you do it.

❏ You tell people they are expected to bring you coffee and get your lunch.

❏ Any idiot knows grunt work is for the grunts.

❏ You make the rules, so you can break them if you want.

❏ You assign others to the menial tasks.

❏ You have the best of everything. The rest of them can use the old stuff.

❏ You believe starting at the bottom is how people pay their dues.

❏ You are not going to ruin your manicure by getting your hands dirty.

❏ No one in your position would ever be seen doing that.

❏ You think it's pretty cool when someone takes a picture of you being just one of the troops. Even better when it hits the media.

❏ You think everyone else is lesser than you, so they can handle the menial work.

❏ You avoid tasks you do not enjoy.

❏ You think it is highly inefficient if a leader spends time doing routine, simple tasks.

❏ You paid your dues long ago. It's someone else's turn.

IMPACT
Risk Factors, Stages & Outcomes

What has already happened or might occur?

❏ A pecking order is established in your organization.

❏ People at the bottom are treated badly.

❏ The worst jobs are dumped on the low-ranking people.

❏ Your role modeling tells people they can reject a job if they feel above it or just don't want to do it.

❏ Tasks are classified on a scale of important to worthless, best to worst, primo to bozo.

❏ No one wants to do the low-level tasks because it is a clear sign of their low rank.

❏ People spend a lot of time trying to prove what they are doing is essential.

❏ People believe if you take the lowly tasks, you will be stuck with them forever.

❏ Job titles clearly indicate your importance in the organization.

❏ People think you believe you are better than everyone else.

❏ People refuse to work for you knowing they are going to start at the bottom (and they have already been there).

❏ Little things do not get done, details are missed, and common tasks are overlooked.

❏ People pit themselves against one another to prove who should rise higher in the hierarchy.

❏ People believe when they attain a certain level, there are perks or work they can avoid.

❏ When there are no people at the bottom, no one does the unwanted tasks.

❏ Some things do not get done. Since you will not do them, they must not be important.

❏ Some people make others look bad so those others will move toward the bottom.

❏ People convince themselves and others that their work is more important than it truly is.

❏ If you break the rules, others have permission to do the same.

❏ People will not confide in you.

❏ You lose perspective on what it is like today to do those essential but unattractive jobs.

★ TREATMENT
Remedy, Prevention & Control

What strategies might work for you? What are you committing to do?

❏ Do the worst job from time to time; it conveys a message of every job is important.

❏ Clearly assign yourself to or volunteer for a low-level task.

❑ Thank people for doing the tough jobs.

❑ Doing something more remedial will remind you of what others are experiencing.

❑ Demonstrate you care by helping someone with an unpleasant task.

❑ Explain how core jobs are the starting point in a process or are essential to a system.

❑ Let someone else take the lead while you assist them.

❑ Create and distribute messages conveying some form of "Every job is important" or "No one is above doing whatever it takes."

❑ Surprise everyone by taking out the trash or making the coffee.

❑ Educate yourself on what it takes to do an unwanted job in order to have a better understanding.

❑ Understand what it means to succeed or fail at a simple or lower job.

❑ Do not think that your once-a-year working the food line or handing out turkeys is a demonstration that you are one of the troops.

❑ Tell individuals that they are important and so is what they do. Be sincere.

❑ Making the sacrifice tells everyone that they should be willing to also sacrifice.

❑ Make a clearer distinction between what you are willing to do and what you need to do.

❑ Explain why certain tasks are important and why you may not be able to do some of them.

❑ Reward people for doing the gritty work.

❑ Recognize the people who are doing the things you are not doing.

NOTES
Observations, Reflections & Conclusions

- Performing tasks or taking responsibilities you are unfamiliar with can provide perspective.

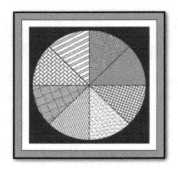

D4. EXOCARDIO

PRONUNCIATION: eks'-oh-kahr'-dee-oh

DEFINITION: Over passionate to your cause. Over dedicated to what you believe is important.

DERIVATION: **EXO** = excess + **CARDIO** = heart

INTERCHANGEABLE WORDS: cause, effort, product, vision, brand, mission, dream, project, event, process, belief, goal

 SYMPTOMS
Signs & Causes

Are you experiencing any of these now or in the past? Which apply to you?

❏ You cannot understand why people are not as committed as you are.

❏ You believe everyone else should think, feel, and act as you do.

❏ You think that everyone will love your idea, immediately embrace it, and begin to work toward the goal.

❏ You sometimes make projects bigger than they need to be.

❏ You expect the other leaders should be at your level of commitment.

❏ In a moment of frustration, you have heard people say, "I am not going to kill myself like you!"

❏ You are disappointed and frustrated that everyone is not taking this as serious as and not working as hard as you.

❏ You are frustrated when people will not make the same sacrifices that you do.

❏ You are surprised or irritated when people back out of commitments.

❏ You believe that the cause would die or diminish significantly without your involvement.

❏ You expect people to volunteer to help when resources are low or stretched.

❏ You believe or assume others have the same passion level as you.

❏ You bring someone onto your team because you gauge their passion to match yours.

❏ You expect people stay later and longer to get the job done.

❏ People complain that you will never be satisfied with their level of commitment.

❏ You want people to be as passionate and committed as you are.

❏ Your values and beliefs are right, and a lot of others have got it wrong.

IMPACT
Risk Factors, Stages & Outcomes

What has already happened or might occur?

❏ People feel they are disappointing you because they are not at the same level of commitment.

❏ You burn yourself out.

❏ People know they cannot rise to your level of dedication, so they reduce their efforts.

❏ People feel that no matter how excited and committed they are, it is never good enough for you.

❏ People fear that if they move to your level, they will be seen as a crazed zealot.

❏ People spend time and energy agonizing whether they should sacrifice at a higher level.

❏ You cannot let go, so you do not move on or over when you should.

❏ People are overwhelmed by the scope and depth of a project.

❏ People quit because they feel their dedication is not or cannot be as high as you want it to be.

❏ Some of your people sacrifice everything, and it takes a toll on them.

❏ People feel like you will put the cause ahead of their needs.

❏ People begin to question your motives because they think you are obsessed.

★ TREATMENT
Remedy, Prevention & Control

What strategies might work for you? What are you committing to do?

❏ Explain why you are so passionate. Be candid and transparent.

❏ Affirm that it is OK for them to be at the level of commitment where they are.

❏ Find out what they are passionate about and integrate it.

❏ Seek their input and ideas and give them credit.

❏ Ask them how they see their passions tying to your or the organization's efforts.

❏ Define to yourself and others what buy-in looks like.

❏ Celebrate major accomplishments of those who are furthering the vision.

❏ Give meaningful pieces of a project to others.

❏ Let them know they are working on something very important and critical.

❏ Tell yourself that they are not in love with it as much as you are, and that's OK.

❏ Help people understand how their passions fit or don't fit with yours.

❏ Determine the levels of commitment by your key people and what balance is needed.

❏ Assess if you really need people or which ones need to be at your level.

❏ Determine if loving the brand, the cause, or the product is essential to success.

❏ If planning for succession, determine the level of dedication and passion needed for a new leader.

❏ Work to heighten people's sensitivity and understanding by education.

❏ Gauge who is at what level and what is truly needed.

❏ Praise those who go above and beyond.

NOTES
Observations, Reflections & Conclusions

• Strongly related to EXPLATONOMY (p. 74) and may lead to RSP (RELASEATPARISIS) (p. 86).

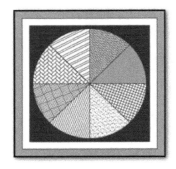

D5. HYPOPIKEMRITIS

PRONUNCIATION: hai'-poh-pik'-um-rai'-tuhs

DEFINITION: Cannot pick or find the right people, put people in wrong places.

DERIVATION: **HYPO** = deficient + **PIK** = pick + **EM** = them + **RITIS** = right

SYMPTOMS
Signs & Causes

Are you experiencing any of these now or in the past? Which apply to you?

- ❏ You stereotype people and make broad assumptions.
- ❏ You tend to believe most people don't really want to do a good job.
- ❏ You feel it is important to keep a significant distance from your people.
- ❏ You will not bring someone on board whom you perceive to be more capable than you.
- ❏ You believe people always fall short or will disappoint you.

❏ You are surprised or shocked at learning something about someone, which you feel you should have known.

❏ You can't seem to get the right people on the bus and in the right seats.

❏ You find yourself avoiding certain people.

❏ You bring in close friends, family, or friends' children.

❏ You have few, if any, deep relationships with your people.

❏ You believe it's very important to establish professional boundaries of work.

❏ You think to yourself, "Never mix work and play."

❏ You use the trial-and-error method to see if someone works out.

❏ You believe "Never get close to your people."

❏ You don't recognize that people have different working styles, communications patterns, and personal needs.

❏ You have the wrong people in the wrong places.

❏ People have said to you, "I don't think you know me very well."

❏ Your people feel they do not have a relationship with you.

❏ You are afraid you will pick the wrong people.

❏ You like to hire more than needed and see who does the best job; then, get rid of the surplus.

❏ You categorize the differences in people as good and bad.

❏ You notice that everyone thinks the same way as you do or always agree.

❑ You wonder why you can never find the right people.

❑ You highly compliment people who are just like you.

❑ You don't surround yourself with strong people.

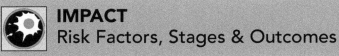

IMPACT
Risk Factors, Stages & Outcomes

What has already happened or might occur?

❑ No one wants to fill the position as your #2 or #3 person.

❑ It is a high probability you will be stuck in your role forever.

❑ Your people are not high quality, and they are not empowered to do their job.

❑ You undervalue or don't understand the capability of your team.

❑ People talk and complain among themselves, therefore reducing productive healthy efforts.

❑ There is a higher incidence of inattention to results and missed opportunities.

❑ People at various levels may question your judgment on the selection or may blame you.

❑ You have no back up for you when you are absent.

❑ Anyone who attempts to fill your role eventually backs off.

❑ People are afraid to have open, honest dialogues.

❑ Getting rid of people becomes easier and easier.

❑ The organization culture does not value the differences among people.

❑ People question their value or contribution because they feel they are different or don't fit in.

❑ No succession plan gets created.

❑ You send a message that you would like everyone to be the same.

❑ People believe the favorites were brought in for no good reason, and they assume they are incapable.

❑ Isolated groups and cliques form.

❑ Without a foundation of healthy relationships, there is a lack of trust among people.

❑ There is a reduction of innovation, risk taking, and experimentation.

❑ What is shared between people is limited, and there is a high level of caution.

❑ Relationships suffer when people feel they are not valued nor heard.

❑ People fear if they do not fit in, they will be gone.

❑ People not working or performing in their area of expertise will not be productive.

★ TREATMENT
Remedy, Prevention & Control

What strategies might work for you? What are you committing to do?

❑ Adopt a policy of "People are good, so let them show it."

❑ Celebrate the positive differences among people.

❑ Have an open conversation of "Do we have the right people in the right places?" Listen.

❑ Ask your people how they see your organization embracing or discouraging diversity.

❑ Make sure that people are effectively connecting to those they lead, their customers, other team members, and all stakeholders.

❑ Send a message that different can be good.

❑ Notice and point out how differences help the efforts.

❑ Focus on your organization's mission and how each person can help fulfill it.

❑ Adopt the slogan: "If you have to get there fast, go alone; if you have to go further, go together."

❑ Continuously improve your selection process.

❑ Evaluate your leadership team. Do you have leaders or managers? Know the differences.

❑ Make sure people are working in the proper lanes.

❑ Ask enough questions to better understand what they know, can do, and want to do.

❑ Let people know what it takes to advance in the organization.

❑ Talk about the future and who can or will be part of it.

❑ Create a succession plan and make sure it is updated as necessary.

 NOTES
Observations, Reflections & Conclusions

- A leader must be authentic in believing that diversity of thought, perspectives, and background is very important.

- It is essential for a leader to recognize the difference between healthy disagreement and incompatibility.
- HYPOPIKEMRITUS (p. 148) has a direct correlation with NOBILDATEAM DISORDER (p. 189).

E. PEOPLE

How you treat those you lead. Interactions, relationships.

Leading people is about mobilizing and optimizing the talent and abilities of others in order to achieve results. Leaders work in environments where people have different views and values, experiences and perceptions, methods, and skills. Leaders must relate and interact. Working with others creates challenges and problems which can easily lead to a leadership disease.

E1. Otrapurfektus

PRONUNCIATION: oh'-truh-puhr-fek'-tuhs

DEFINITION: Expect others to be perfect, to not fail or make mistakes.

DERIVATION: **OTRA** = others + **PURFEK** = perfect + **TUS** + for us

SYMPTOMS
Signs & Causes

Are you experiencing any of these now or in the past? Which apply to you?

❏ You set expectations that are nearly impossible to meet.

❏ People are fired or asked to leave when mistakes are made or goals missed.

❏ You find yourself using phrases like "That was a bone head mistake" or "Only stupid people make mistakes."

❏ People cover up their mistakes.

❏ People criticize and blame others to deflect from themselves.

❑ People do not like to speak up in meetings.

❑ New ideas or ways of doing are seldom presented.

❑ Since you work constantly and ignore other aspects of your life, you want others to do the same.

❑ Planning goals are intentionally set very high but difficult to reach.

❑ You don't understand why something was not done; you could have done it with one hand tied behind your back.

❑ People seem afraid to admit mistakes.

❑ Change is not happening very often.

❑ Failure is a word you do not like to hear, and everyone knows it.

❑ Since you set high expectations and lofty goals for yourself, you expect others to do the same.

❑ New products and services seldom get launched.

❑ You hear people complaining they do not have the resources, time, or information needed to excel.

❑ You hear yourself or others talking strongly about financial loss when something goes wrong.

❑ People miss quotas and deadlines constantly.

❑ When the question of "How did this happen?" is asked, everyone is silent.

❑ You come down on failure hard.

IMPACT
Risk Factors, Stages & Outcomes

What has already happened or might occur?

❑ There is no opportunity to learn from mistakes.

❑ Someone takes the blame (rightly or wrongly) and becomes the scapegoat.

❑ People are afraid to set a high goal for fear of not being able to achieve it.

❑ Time is devoted to the unproductive activity of hiding and covering mistakes.

❑ The abilities and contributions of people who leave are lost from the team.

❑ People take responsibilities on or start projects feeling hopeless about attaining success.

❑ People are distracted by your focus on what they are not doing right.

❑ People are afraid to or do not like to experiment or try something new or different.

❑ People want to hear how the leader defines failure before they act.

❑ People blame someone else in order to shift the attention from themselves.

❑ People leave feeling they have made too many mistakes or could not meet expectations.

❑ People are very careful to not be associated with someone who is labeled as flawed.

❑ People are often fearful to take credit in case failure is assigned to their efforts.

❑ Following what is modeled by the leader, others contract this disease.

❑ People may burn out and some explosively, leaving a wake of damage behind them.

❑ People create unhealthy ways of competing to look good or better than others.

❏ Your heavy emotional investment leads to exhaustion, frustration, and/or irritation.

❏ People do not grow in their roles because they are not learning how to solve their own problems.

❏ Your intention for everyone to succeed becomes unhealthy when people are unwilling to pay the price for being perfect and making no mistakes.

★ TREATMENT
Remedy, Prevention & Control

What strategies might work for you? What are you committing to do?

❏ Give people the freedom to try new things.

❏ Quit talking about not making mistakes.

❏ Encourage people to take risks. Create a culture of "Risks are OK."

❏ Convert your expectation of perfection into a set of high standards.

❏ Assure that goals and standards are clear and achievable.

❏ Help people understand the balance of *failure is not all bad and not all good either.*

❏ Promote intelligent discoveries.

❏ Encourage and reward curiosity. We are not looking for the perfect answer, but we may discover something new by being curious.

❏ Communicate to others that it is all right to make a mistake, and that you will help them learn and improve.

❏ Ask people what is keeping them from doing a better job or excelling.

❏ Ask questions which invite people to utilize a process of careful thought.

❏ Make it OK to try something new or different.

❏ Prevent or protect people from distractions. This allows them to stay focused.

❏ Facilitate a conversation to analyze why something worked (or didn't) and what was learned.

❏ Insist on disagreement or dissent – at least alternate ideas.

❏ Realize that failures of a system or organization are usually caused by process or communication failures and not the staff intentionally failing.

❏ Start by asking questions and collecting more data and information.

❏ Hold your judgment until all the facts are in and you have heard from ALL parties.

❏ Demonstrate that you are interested in truth and facts.

❏ Do not favor one party over the other as having more valuable information than another.

❏ Realize that failure is really the tuition paid on the way to success.

❏ Ask yourself, if this fails, can we handle the fallout?

❏ If something fails or is not perfect, think ahead how you will handle accusations, jokes, criticisms.

❏ Study the innovation process and how it can be used in your organization.

❏ Be inspired by the stories of failure turned into success.

❑ Ask your people, "What am I doing to place you in a position to fail." Then fix it.

❑ Provide safe harbor for people to make mistakes by showing how you make mistakes.

❑ Look for positive intent. Almost no one comes to work wanting to screw up.

❑ Take the time to discover what someone was expecting to happen. Acknowledge their try.

❑ Talk about how to make a different decision or take a different action next time.

NOTES
Observations, Reflections & Conclusions

• If a leader has the disease of SUPRAPERFEKTUS (p. 60), that leader may also have OTRAPERFEKTUS (p. 172).

• It is easy for a leader with OTRAPERFEKTUS (p. 172) to contract BCT (BLAMCRITONOMY) (p. 178).

E2. BCT (BLAMCRITONOMY)

PRONUNCIATION: blaym'-krih-tah'-nuh-mee

DEFINITION: Criticizes others and blames others.

DERIVATION: **BLAM** = blame + **CRI** = criticize + **TON** = heavy weight + **OMY** = act or process of cutting

INTERCHANGEABLE WORDS: Group A (verbs): blame, criticize, fault, chastise, condemn, denounce, bash, disparage, slam, reprimand, resist, demand, complain. Group B (nouns): deficiency, inadequacy, guilt, rejection, demand, adversary, enemy, fault.

SYMPTOMS
Signs & Causes

Are you experiencing any of these now or in the past? Which apply to you?

- ❑ You condemn leaders or people who are on the other side of an issue.

- ❑ You get angry when people complain about you.

- ❑ You deflect from your mistakes or inadequacies.

- ❑ You know hard lessons are the best ones. They sink in deeper.

❑ Deep in your heart, you know something was at least partially your fault, but you want the blame to land on someone else.

❑ You have great difficulty acknowledging good in people. You primarily or mostly focus on the negative.

❑ You spend most of your time with people who are *not* doing well giving you plenty to criticize or blame.

❑ You really don't care if people get mad at you.

❑ You ask questions that are impossible to answer.

❑ When you overhear, "I just got royally chewed out!" you know they are talking about you.

❑ You believe if people are not told what they are doing wrong, they will never learn.

❑ You are often harsh with your feedback.

❑ You do not try to understand why someone did what they did.

❑ You believe if you make others look bad, they won't see your deficiencies.

❑ On the bathroom wall someone wrote, "_____ is a jerk," and your name was in the blank. (The word jerk may be replaced by a variety of less complimentary words.)

❑ You do not care how people feel or what they are experiencing.

❑ You frequently use the phrase "I told you so" (or some form of it).

❑ You believe people are the problem, and it is seldom the system that is at fault.

❑ You seldom intervene when failure is about to happen as it gives you someone to blame.

❏ You generally do not like the way others do things.

❏ People believe and say that you are impossible to please.

❏ You like to take credit for what went well and find fault with others on what went poorly.

IMPACT
Risk Factors, Stages & Outcomes

What has already happened or might occur?

❏ People feel like they did what they were supposed to, and it still fell apart.

❏ People believe you have no compassion or empathy.

❏ Others model your behavior by criticizing and blaming.

❏ People speculate (or know) you are covering your mistakes.

❏ When you step in, a dark cloud hangs over everything, and you are the thunderstorm.

❏ Your people's health (physical and mental) is impacted in negative ways.

❏ There is high turnover in your organization or on your team.

❏ People are highly stressed and fearful of making mistakes.

❏ Your people spend time trying to support others and repair the damage you inflicted upon them.

❏ The confidence of your people drops.

❏ People describe the environment around you as negative or toxic.

❏ Complaints to human resources increase.

❏ People do everything they can to cover mistakes, failures, and problems.

❏ People realize that you created the system or structure which is causing the negative results.

❏ You are unable to recognize it may be the organization or process that has failed.

❏ It gets around the community that "No one wants to work for that jerk" (and you are the jerk).

❏ People avoid interacting with you at any cost.

❏ People feel they have to withhold facts out of fear.

❏ You are blindsided by people who give up or quit.

❏ Your stress level increases due to excess negativity that you are creating.

❏ Staff do not approach you with problems. Difficulties are hidden.

⭐ TREATMENT
Remedy, Prevention & Control

What strategies might work for you? What are you committing to do?

❏ Recognize it may not be anyone's fault; it could be something else.

❏ Analyze how your systems or processes may be creating or perpetuating problems.

❏ Ask yourself, "Has something changed in our environment making it difficult for people to succeed?"

❏ Forgive your critics allowing you to let go of bad feelings which are holding you back or keeping you in a negative place.

❏ Do not start a meeting with a gripe or complaint. Begin with compliments and positive recognition.

❏ Ask this question at the end of each day: "Who did I treat today in a manner I am not pleased with?"

❏ When you identify something that you need to correct, make a note to yourself and do it.

❏ When you have wronged someone, find that person the next day and apologize in person. If not possible to do so, call; do not text or send an email.

❏ As part of that conversation, ask how you could do better.

❏ Consider first if the problem is due to something which is *not* people based.

❏ Look deeply at why you are so critical and prone to blame others.

❏ Analyze if people are doing simply what the system wants, expects, or requires.

❏ Adopt a lower stress lifestyle: meditate, exercise, yoga, and/or journal things you appreciate; do so daily!

❏ After a negative interaction, "If the same was done to me, would I be angry?"

❏ Hold people accountable, but do not crush them. It's a balancing act.

❏ Explore what your role was in a bad outcome and accept responsibility for your part.

❏ Share the credit when things go well and take the blame when things go badly.

❏ Apologize when you unfairly criticize or blame.

❏ Realize that your improved handling of people serves as a role model for how to change and what to do better.

❑ Make yourself vulnerable, admit you are wrong, and ask how to move past problems together.

❑ Admit to your people that you have become aware of doing too much criticizing and blaming.

❑ Announce that you are going to attempt to change and take steps to create a better environment.

❑ Ask for others' help in making positive change. Set some parameters for what would be helpful to everyone involved.

❑ Use role playing in a workshop or professional development session to learn how to better handle your urges and actions.

❑ Focus on individuals rather than an entire group.

 NOTES
Observations, Reflections & Conclusions

- There is a significant correlation with this disease and SUPRAPERFEKTUS (p. 60) and OTRAPERFEKTUS (p. 172).

- In many cases, a leader may have all three conditions at the same time.

- If leaders never accept responsibility for blaming and criticizing, they may develop a victim mentality from the reactions of others to their actions.

E3. **AVCO** (**Avoconflikto**)

Pronunciation: ah'-voh-kuhn-flik'-toh

Definition: Avoids or deflects conflict. Inability to manage or handle it.

Derivation: **AVO**id + **CONFLIK** = conflict + **TO** = action or condition suggestive of movement

Interchangeable Words: dispute, quarrel, squabble, disagreement, difference of opinion, dissension discord, friction, strife, contention, clash, exchange, tussle, schism

SYMPTOMS
Signs & Causes

Are you experiencing any of these now or in the past? Which apply to you?

- ❏ You find it very uncomfortable to handle conflict.

- ❏ As soon as a conflict begins, you tune out or walk away.

- ❏ You find yourself in the middle of nearly every disagreement.

- ❏ You say or do things that your followers disagree with strongly.

❑ You want everyone to like you.

❑ You often find yourself as judge between competing parties.

❑ People think if you get involved, it will just get worse.

❑ You find yourself agreeing with everyone even though they are on different sides.

❑ You cannot, will not, or are unable to balance priorities for yourself or others.

❑ You avoid conflict situations with people or handle them poorly.

❑ You want everyone to get along and be one big happy family.

❑ It seems like there is a lot of gossip in your organization.

❑ You feel that the parties will remain firm in their thoughts and beliefs no matter what you try.

❑ You often realize you have picked the weak or wrong side of a conflict.

❑ Believing it is good for the organization or team, you like to stir things up from time to time.

❑ You do not understand how experiences and perspectives shape people's thinking.

❑ You have a difficult time grasping who is in which group.

❑ You think it is a good idea to keep one foot in each camp.

❑ If you secretly looked into your soul, you actually enjoy when there is conflict.

❑ People wonder why you cannot see or understand disagreements.

❑ You avoid difficult conversations.

❏ You try to smooth things out and please everyone.

❏ You think that all parties will remain firm in their positions no matter what you do.

 IMPACT
Risk Factors, Stages & Outcomes

What has already happened or might occur?

❏ People interpret your avoidance as a lack of confidence.

❏ People do not follow your leadership because they think you are inept.

❏ People believe you are unwilling to respond and are perhaps afraid.

❏ People believe that you do not have the ability to manage or handle conflict.

❏ People are confused by competing interests, perspectives, and goals.

❏ Consensus cannot be reached, and conflicts stall or escalate.

❏ Poor communication up front, fear of conflict, and people pleasing create one big mess!

❏ When you are forced to handle conflict, no one wants to listen to you or follow your lead.

❏ Conflicts get worse and expand into other areas.

❏ A culture of tolerance for disruptive people is created.

❏ Perceiving you are weak and cannot handle critical conflicts, you lose your position or are kicked out.

❏ Differences are viewed as triggers for conflict.

❏ The intensity of conflicts increases.

❑ You feel caught in the middle.

❑ You are afraid to decide or lead a process thinking if it fails, it will be your fault.

❑ Good people leave because of unresolved differences.

❑ You are paralyzed by the conflict. You have no clue what to do.

❑ You are seen as a fence sitter.

❑ You support one side and alienate those in the opposite position.

❑ People fabricate, speculate, and assume due to poor communication about a conflict.

★ TREATMENT
Remedy, Prevention & Control

What strategies might work for you? What are you committing to do?

❑ Agree to disagree.

❑ Realize you cannot please everyone, and that is OK.

❑ Be flexible, nimble, and adaptable.

❑ Learn how to be an effective facilitator.

❑ Improve your active listening skills.

❑ Convene or pull groups or people together to talk and listen to each other.

❑ Find common ground.

❑ Remain calm during the storm.

❑ Realize that conflict is a natural part of change.

❑ Try to understand all sides measured by your ability to explain all perspectives.

❏ Balance all constituencies.

❏ Define your role. Are you part of the conflict or are you a mediator?

❏ Recognize that all sides were created by the experiences and beliefs of the people in each corner.

❏ Practice role playing with someone who can give you constructive tips.

❏ Demonstrate respect and protect people's dignity.

❏ Listen to each version or unique perspective of involved parties.

❏ Define who the parties are and what their position is.

❏ Determine who actually has a stake in this conflict and who has inserted themselves inappropriately.

❏ Realize that being heard is in itself therapeutic.

❏ Validate what you hear by repeating it back until you get it.

❏ Tell yourself that conflict is not bad. It is a process which needs to be managed.

❏ Find the common goal and allow each side to pursue it their way.

❏ Give and receive corrective criticism as a way to work through conflicts.

❏ Take a course in conflict resolution.

NOTES
Observations, Reflections & Conclusions

- Conflict has many forms, a myriad of causalities, and a wide variety of intensity levels.
- Conflict can be between two parties or hundreds.

E4. NOBILDATEAM DISORDER

PRONUNCIATION: noh-bihl'-duh-teem'

DEFINITION: Cannot build an effective team or positive culture. Unable to create and nurture constructive relationships between you and others.

DERIVATION: **NO** + **BILD** = build + **A** + **TEAM DISORDER** = relatively distinct condition resulting from dysfunction.

INTERCHANGEABLE WORDS: Since a team is defined as a group of individuals working together to achieve a goal, teams are also committees, boards, task forces, project groups, etc.

SYMPTOMS
Signs & Causes

Are you experiencing any of these now or in the past? Which apply to you?

❑ You do not know how to engage people in meaningful ways.

❑ People seem detached or distant from what is occurring or needs to happen.

❑ You view people problems, input, and capacity as constraints which are disposable.

❏ Everyone on your team seems to be the same or very similar.

❏ You assume everyone is motivated by the same things or in the same ways.

❏ You believe you have the magic formula for motivating people.

❏ You wonder why new people struggle to become part of the team.

❏ You have publicly disagreed with your team.

❏ You feel like you do not know your people very well.

❏ You have tried everything, and you still don't have a team.

❏ You frequently hear people complaining about their team.

❏ It takes a big effort on your part to build a relationship with individuals.

❏ Although together for a while, your team does not know each other very well.

❏ Your organization does not test, evaluate, or assess people before joining your teams.

❏ You find it quite difficult to describe three personal facts about each of your people.

❏ It takes a long time for you to get to know new people.

❏ You were seldom or never part of any teams when you were younger.

❏ You have some people who can't get along with others and you have given up on them.

❏ It seems to take forever for a person to become part of the team.

❏ You have said "I really don't have a very good team."

❑ You notice that everyone thinks the same way or always agrees.

❑ You hear this complaint: "He doesn't do it the way the rest of us do."

❑ Someone told you that you really embarrassed the team.

❑ When you look at diversity, it's only about gender, age, and skin color.

❑ You are not very good at sizing people up.

❑ People make fun of certain team members.

❑ You have no clue what a stakeholder analysis is, let alone how to do one.

❑ You like the concept of "People are followers, like sheep, and you are the shepherd."

❑ You are not sure if you can trust your team to function without your guidance.

❑ You have read all types of books on team building, and you still cannot figure it out.

IMPACT
Risk Factors, Stages & Outcomes

What has already happened or might occur?

❑ People are assigned to a team without you or the team knowing much about them.

❑ Team members cannot describe each other's background, knowledge, skills, or experience.

❑ You know little about your team members and what makes them tick.

❑ A culture of tolerance for ineffective or disruptive people is created.

❏ No one can define the terms collaboration or consensus.

❏ Your team feels outside of what is going on or that what they are doing is not important.

❏ People do not understand how life experience and background is part of diversity.

❏ Someone, other than you, assumes the role of team leader.

❏ Team members do not get what they need; therefore, they do not try and eventually withdraw.

❏ There is stress on everyone, and it negatively impacts what they are trying to achieve.

❏ Extra effort is needed to keep a team motivated and focused.

❏ You and your people do not know how to develop a team's unique collective talents.

❏ Teams complain about each other or complain about other teams and groups.

❏ People are forced to conform or get pushed out.

❏ People do not draw on the talents of each other.

❏ People avoid interacting with specific people or anyone on their team.

❏ The team is embarrassed, and morale is damaged.

❏ Your favorites are given best assignments or easy tasks.

❏ People feel you do not trust their team to execute on goals.

❏ Dysfunction unwittingly creates a toxic team.

❏ Discontent and worries grow among the team about its ability to perform.

❑ You will never have a *dream team*.

❑ Teams explode over dissatisfaction and dysfunctionality.

❑ Coworkers are not respectful to each other.

❑ People feel that the teammates do not really care about them or *have their back*.

★ TREATMENT
Remedy, Prevention & Control

What strategies might work for you? What are you committing to do?

❑ Believe in your people. Believe that they ultimately want to do a good job.

❑ Offer activities where people can get to know each other.

❑ Realize individuals respond to different approaches for communication, relationships, and learning. Figure out who needs what.

❑ Improve your facilitation and small group process skills.

❑ Take time to remind yourself that your team is functioning well and enjoy it.

❑ Celebrate what people have in common. That is what binds them.

❑ Reflect on what each person needs, especially the ones who need extra attention.

❑ Brag publicly and privately about your team when it's working and sometimes when it's not.

❑ Build team members who have the ability to supplement or replace you.

❑ Relish improvements when things are working well.

❑ Remind yourself team building takes time and every time you lose or add someone, the process begins again.

❑ Realize that it is a compliment to your leadership when your team is successful.

❑ Continually remind your team that having diverse backgrounds, perspectives, and experiences is good.

❑ Look at your team as a group of leaders or potential leaders.

❑ Be intentional about creating time and space to talk with your team about solutions to move forward.

❑ Create a team atmosphere where credit is shared and blame banished.

❑ Do not underestimate how culture and team can have an enormous impact on your outcomes.

❑ Keep a balance between your individual goals and the team's goals.

❑ Make sure people believe the goal can be achieved collectively.

❑ Recognize differences in a positive way and celebrate those differences.

❑ Balance the needs of different units or audiences within the organization.

❑ Attend social activities which involve your team members.

❑ Focus on the positive aspects of teamwork and the natural evolution of teams.

❑ Do not spend extensive time devoted to normal mood changes and common interactive struggles.

❑ Ask your people how they define *an authentic relationship.*

❑ Recognize and reward positive teamwork.

❑ Do not be afraid to fire volunteers if they are not good for the team.

NOTES
Observations, Reflections & Conclusions

• Culture and team are highly interrelated concepts.

• Culture is defined as a set of shared beliefs, attitudes, knowledge, practices, and behaviors.

E5. TRAINEMPHRAXIS

PRONUNCIATION: tray'-nuhm-frak'-sihs

DEFINITION: Don't train, teach, empower, assist, support, equip, or prepare others. Cannot effectively convey expectations.

DERIVATION: **TRAIN** + **EM**power + **PHRAXIS** = stoppage or obstruction

INTERCHANGEABLE WORDS: teach, train, present, instruct, build, empower, encourage, assist, support, mentor, demonstrate, coach, tutor.

SYMPTOMS
Signs & Causes

Are you experiencing any of these now or in the past? Which apply to you?

❏ You promise something needed, but do not provide it.

❏ You teach the same way to everyone assuming they all learn the same way, and then you wonder why some do not get it.

❏ You hear people say, "I didn't understand that's what you expected."

❑ Your organization does not have an orientation program or an **onboarding** process.

❑ You do not understand why people don't get it the first time.

❑ When frustrated you say, "You asked me to help you and now you are complaining."

❑ When people don't do it exactly the way you taught them, you consider it was done wrong.

❑ You hear people say to you, "You are not listening to me."

❑ You think you are not very good at teaching or showing people how to do.

❑ You really enjoy working with those who appreciate you or those you like.

❑ You forget to use words of encouragement when people are succeeding.

❑ You believe with the right tools and a little instruction; people should be able to figure out what to do.

❑ You publicly point out an individual's mistakes as an example of what not to do.

❑ People frequently complain, "Nobody told me" or "Nobody let me know."

❑ Your frustration shows easily when others are struggling to learn.

❑ You think it's important to point out when people mess up.

❑ You are not sure what to do when you are helping people, and they don't get it.

❑ You believe people should ask questions if they don't know.

❏ You are so proud of yourself when people succeed. It was all because of you.

❏ You believe it helps and motivates others when their errors are made public.

❏ You hear people say, "I wish they would have told me that from the beginning."

❏ When others suggest a better way to learn/teach, you dismiss their ideas.

❏ You say, "There is no such thing as a stupid question, until someone asks a stupid question."

❏ You seldom ask anyone else to train or teach others. You can do it better than anyone.

❏ You are supportive of only those who are working hard and doing it right.

❏ People often respond to you with, "I *did* do what you asked.

❏ You expect others to jump in and perform new tasks and procedures with no opportunity to practice.

IMPACT
Risk Factors, Stages & Outcomes

What has already happened or might occur?

❏ Your people do not know what to do or what you expect.

❏ Motivation and morale in the organization or on the team drop.

❏ People have to figure it out for themselves and therefore cannot perform until they do.

❏ People are highly frustrated by not knowing what and how to do something.

❑ People think, "Why should I help you; you never help me."

❑ There is very little loyalty to you.

❑ Time is wasted. Inefficiency is high due to poor preparation and ineffective training.

❑ Outcomes are negative and unanticipated or not what is needed.

❑ You become very upset at the lack of execution.

❑ People are hesitant to help others or teach them.

❑ People have great difficulty connecting the dots from knowledge to performance.

❑ Your people do not talk to or show you what they are learning.

❑ Overall performance suffers.

❑ People feel you do not care about them.

★ TREATMENT
Remedy, Prevention & Control

What strategies might work for you? What are you committing to do?

❑ Ask your people what tools, skills, and information they need to do their job.

❑ Look for model systems that empower people to pursue a vision or do their job.

❑ Ask your people "What can I do to help you?" Listen, understand, then deliver.

❑ Role model that learning and growth are important and the key to success.

❑ Become a lifelong learner and tell people how and why you made that commitment.

❏ Share specific, positive, and constructive feedback.

❏ Use the *2 for 1 Rule*: provide two positive comments at the same time you offer one which may be perceived as negative.

❏ Create a comprehensive orientation or onboarding process for new people.

❏ Ask, "What would help you learn better?"

❏ Give clear instructions and ask if people understand. Note their non-verbal response.

❏ Make sure expectations, outcomes, and consequences are clear, even written, from the start.

❏ Explain what success looks like to you.

❏ Ask an abundance of clarifying questions.

❏ Recognize and reward people for learning, not just performing.

❏ Teach others how to teach others.

❏ After a few weeks, ask new people what could have been done better to help them perform.

❏ Assign mentors to everyone.

❏ Ask questions rather than give directives.

❏ Find creative ways to celebrate success.

❏ Do not assume people understand you or you understand them. Check and validate.

❏ Create written procedures, processes, and practices.

❏ If people are not learning and growing, assume the fault is yours, not theirs.

❏ Do not expect people to read between the lines. Don't leave room for them to do so.

❏ Evaluate the circumstances which cause people to fail.

❑ Take learning styles and talent strengths into consideration when assignments are made.

❑ Once you delegate or describe what you want them to do, ask them to paraphrase their understanding back to you. Clarify.

NOTES
Observations, Reflections & Conclusions

- TRAINEMPHRAXIS (p. 196) can have strong correlations with HYPERMANAGITUS (p. 148) and NDG (p. 142).

E6. NOREC
(NORECREWAPHASIA)

PRONUNCIATION: noh-rehk'-ree-wah-fai'-zhee-uh

DEFINITION: Do not recognize, appreciate, or reward people. Fail to celebrate victory or triumph.

DERIVATION: **NO** + **REC**ognition + **REW**ard + **APHASIA** = partial or total loss of ability to communicate

INTERCHANGEABLE WORDS: thank, recognize, appreciate, reward, compliment, award, praise

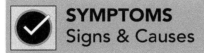

SYMPTOMS
Signs & Causes

Are you experiencing any of these now or in the past? Which apply to you?

❑ People tell you, "You should have recognized this person for (fill in the blank), but you didn't."

❑ As you walk away from someone who has done something for you, you hear them mutter "A thanks would have been nice."

❑ You still don't understand what motivates people.

❏ You are not much of a tipper.

❏ You do not say "Thank you" very often.

❏ You believe only weak people need to be recognized and appreciated.

❏ Recognizing your *favorite* people is what you do.

❏ You tell individuals privately that they did a good job, but you seldom tell anyone else about it.

❏ Incentives never seem to work for you.

❏ You think "No one rewards, recognizes, or appreciates you, so why should you do it for them."

❏ You are not sure why people need to be praised when they are successful.

❏ You tell people, "If you want appreciation, find it in the dictionary" or something similar.

❏ When things are not getting done, you just want to yell, "Just do your job."

❏ You thank the wrong person or give credit to people who didn't actually do the work.

❏ When two or more people are successful, you praise one but not the others.

❏ People say that you never say anything good about anybody.

❏ No matter what you try, your motivation methods do not seem to work.

❏ You forget to recognize someone who has done something worth noting.

❏ You believe an accomplishment should be a reward in itself.

❏ You think that the only reward that motivates people is money.

IMPACT
Risk Factors, Stages & Outcomes

What has already happened or might occur?

- ❏ People feel unappreciated.
- ❏ Because you do not seem to care for people, others may not care about you.
- ❏ People feel they are being used.
- ❏ People do the minimal or just what they have to do.
- ❏ Motivation is low or non-existent.
- ❏ People think you don't appreciate anything.
- ❏ People leave and go to places where they are rewarded and appreciated.
- ❏ You seldom receive positive comments about you or your efforts.
- ❏ People do not work very hard or put forth a good effort. They think "Why should I?"
- ❏ People feel you don't care about them.
- ❏ People play games and try to win your favor so they will be rewarded.
- ❏ Productivity is not optimized.
- ❏ There is little pride in the work being done.

TREATMENT
Remedy, Prevention & Control

What strategies might work for you? What are you committing to do?

- ❏ Ask others to tell you who is being overlooked for a compliment or recognition.

❑ Celebrate success and honor those who played a role in it.

❑ Say thank you as often as you can or set a goal of thank you's for each day.

❑ Make heroes of people who engage in constructive conversation and dialog.

❑ Give credit to those who deserve it. Be generous with praise.

❑ Give away something that everyone knows is valuable to you.

❑ Find something good to say to the one or two people you seldom praise.

❑ Recognize performance even when it is not great. That person put out an effort or was really trying.

❑ Be regular, even schedule times, with thanks, recognition, appreciation, and praise.

❑ Tie recognition and reward to clear measurable results.

❑ Ask others to step forward for recognition while you step back.

❑ Adopt a motto of "Credit is shared, and blame banished."

❑ Ask people to tell you who helped them be successful, then recognize those people.

❑ Make sure positive recognition is public.

❑ Ask people individually what they consider a reward for themselves.

❑ Hand out some token item which you always carry a supply with you.

❑ When questioning if you should include someone for recognition, err on the side of inclusion.

❑ Visit an out of the way or seldom visited place and say thanks.

❑ With your own hands, make a tangible award which you can present to people.

❑ Be consistent with your rewards.

❑ Ask others if they feel you fairly distribute reward and appreciation.

❑ Recognize and appreciate those who are not extraordinary but are working hard and doing their job day after day.

 NOTES
Observations, Reflections & Conclusions

- There are many similarities between NOREC (p. 202) and TRAINEMPHRAXIS (p. 196). Look closely at the symptoms to differentiate.

PATH TO BECOMING A HEALTHY LEADER

So, you have now looked through all of the diseases and have reached some conclusions, or perhaps, have more questions. You may find yourself with these thoughts:

- You wonder if you have picked the right ones for yourself.
- You think you are currently infected with several but have had all the rest at some point.
- You believe you have contracted quite a few of these but have thankfully recovered and are much healthier now.
- You are concerned that you have experienced some but are not sure if you are healed.
- You are afraid there are several diseases you have not had and dread the day they infect you.
- You believe your analysis of everyone else is perfect, yet you have not had the courage to diagnose yourself.
- You believe you have no diseases and never have, which means you are in denial and that is a human mental health problem.

Note: Some of you may think you have nearly all of them, which is probably not true. If it were, you most likely would have no roles in leadership.

If you are recognizing and acknowledging your diseases, a second set of questions arise:

- What do you need to do now?
- Do you have too many?
- How severe are those you have contracted?
- Do you address them all at once or one at a time?

At this point it becomes a process of creating criteria and strategies to prioritize most pressing, biggest impact, most common, most difficult, or easiest to remedy.

This portion of this book is designed to answer your questions, stimulate your thinking, help you reach conclusions, and analyze your strategies.

Were You Able to Self-Diagnose?

How successful were you at diagnosing yourself? Have you invested the needed time and effort to truly discover your condition? Can you recognize your symptoms and signs? Are you able to acknowledge the impact the disease is already having on you? Are you willing to take it seriously?

Did you consult with others? Was their participation at your request or was it prompted by someone else? In other words, have you integrated a measure of objectivity to validate, challenge, or cross check your findings?

Were you focusing on yourself or on other leaders? Of course, it is easier to see the leadership health deficiencies of others. You witness leaders who are not performing well, seem distracted, have lost energy and drive, are out of sorts, or not the same as they used to be. When you are inside the bubble of your own leadership world, it is more difficult to see these in yourself.

The process of diagnosis has two stages: **assessment**, then **acknowledgement**. Both can be difficult. You must first be willing to assess. An assessment can come from you and/ or it can be provided by others. As you analyze the disease checklists, you will need to examine the scope, intensity, and range of your symptoms and the impact they are having on you. It is important to be open to what it all means.

The acknowledgement stage happens when you are able to face the truth about yourself, address your problems, and admit your fears. The checklist in each disease chapter may stimulate you to read and research more as you seek an understanding of yourself. Facing the reality of what your symptoms may mean can be quite difficult.

If you found yourself checking a large number of boxes for a specific disease or several of the diseases, you may be quite leadersick. The impact on you or your people may have already begun and may be even more significant into the future. Do not be overwhelmed by the feelings you are having or deterred by the assumptions you are making. The vast majority of diagnoses are not fatal and the end to your leadership.

Most importantly, take charge of your diagnosis and the actions needed to remedy your situation. A diagnosis should be considered the beginning of your journey toward recovery and growth and the opportunity for you to become a healthier leader.

A note of caution to consider. Most of us can usually tell when we are sick. But there are times we cannot. We may be ignoring symptoms or not realizing their importance as in, "Oh, this is just normal" or "I'll get over it." Or, you have self-diagnosed incorrectly and embarked upon treatment. At that point, you could be in trouble. That is why engaging others is important.

Role of Others in Diagnosis

Most leaders will utilize other people to help in their diagnosis. They are rich resources of experience and knowledge. Others can see and hear what you may not, observe your actions, reference your background, and know how and what you think. They can be more objective; although, if they are friends, there may be some level of bias.

When you engage others, you need to find people you trust, individuals who you are willing to listen to and learn from. You must give them permission to speak candidly. They need to feel safe, believing their input will not meet with repercussions, damage, loss of friendship or status, or limited access to you. They must not fear penalties through overt or covert punishment. Realize they are taking a risk by honestly sharing with you. It can be a test of your relationship.

As you absorb their input, acknowledge the effort they have made. Be appreciative of their investments of time. Most likely, they are helping you because they care and want you to be a better leader. Their wisdom and advice may be the difference between an incorrect diagnosis or even missing some symptoms completely. If they are with you through the early stages, they may be of greater help in the long run.

You may experience people saying you have a specific disease which you do not understand or with which you might even disagree. To analyze the validity of the diagnosis, consider the source. Is this someone for whom you have great respect and admiration? Is it an individual who you feel is wise and experienced? Is it a person who believes in you and wants the best for you? If you can answer any or all of these questions with a "Yes," you most likely have a person who will be of great help. If you view the input as solid, you should take it seriously.

Note: There are ways to obtain feedback and input by allowing people to be anonymous. Using the checklists, allow others to evaluate you against the symptoms and impacts.

 LeadersickBook.com/checklists/ provides the checklists in forms which you can download, or you may copy them from your book. There are also instructions on how to use them. Allowing multiple people to complete the forms will provide a broader base of input.

Being a Seeker

Most of us have heard the term *health nuts*. It is a term used to describe people who are obsessed with their health. How about *fitness freaks*? They are the ones who are fixated on exercise and keeping fit. They share a passion, determination, and commitment to a high level of being healthy and in shape.

In the arenas of management and psychology, we use terms like self-improvement, growth mindset, emotional intelligence, and self-actualization. These concepts promote the idea of a person who seeks to personally reach higher, improve, and achieve more. My favorite term to associate with this kind of person is *life-long learning*, constantly searching for knowledge to fuel that internal growth.

Curiosity is one of the most common characteristics of successful leaders. It is a nearly insatiable desire to learn. Challenges, problems, and questions are primarily addressed by actions which nourish a need to understand. When this trait is applied to self, it becomes the driving force to recognize and comprehend every aspect of a leadership disease.

In medical terms, curiosity can be compared to the lungs, constantly operating with an in-and-out motion. The lungs need air like a leader needs knowledge. As a body is pushed or exerted, the body has an increased need for oxygen making the lungs work harder. When a leadership disease has seriously affected someone in a leadership role, there is an expanded need for information on what is happening, what is its impact, and what can be done to address it.

The road to recovery in health care is more effective when a patient adopts a desire to learn. People who have illnesses become seekers who are researching, reading, asking questions, listening to advice, and absorbing the experience of others.

Keep reading, listening, and watching. You may never have it all figured out, but there is always something new to learn. The commitment to being a seeker helps leaders (and those who depend on them) grow and, in the context of leadership diseases, heal.

Commitment to Change & Improvement

Acknowledging your weaknesses and failures is not easy, but admitting you have a disease may be tougher. It means you must put a significant effort into learning about the disease, determining how and why you have it, understanding the impact it is having on you and those you lead, creating a treatment plan, and going through the process of healing and recovery.

With a weakness, it is usually about how to work around it or try to overcome it as best you can. With a failure you learn from it, address it, and move forward. Sometimes, we allow failure to continually damage us and disrupt our journey in life. Failure and weakness are inherent in many of the leadership diseases.

Recovery from a leadership disease requires you to want to change and be willing to do the work necessary for improvement. Knowing the issues and having the ability to do the hard work are two different processes. Once you become aware of the disease, you must be committed to making the sacrifices to overcome the illness.

Many of the treatments in this book revolve around the need to continually gain knowledge, refine your healing practices, and have the right attitude. Again, this is a common calling for everyone, not just leaders. Yet if you neglect to learn and grow, you will have greater difficulty in healing.

You must make a commitment to dedicate the time needed to learn and change. In addition, understanding and accepting your challenges and failures are parts of your leadership health journey. If a leader abides by the formula for good leadership health -- practicing integrity, honesty, and trust -- it will be much easier to acknowledge and develop through weaknesses, challenges, and mistakes.

The most important characteristic for leaders to address leadership diseases is the commitment to learning. Learning about what the diseases are, how they are contracted, and how to recognize the signs. You must also understand the impact and progress of the disease on you and others, then consider and implement treatment and prevention. A common mistake of many leaders is to disregard their leadership health by thinking it is not important, and therefore continuous learning for them is not important.

It is important to note that strong personalities and engrained habits are difficult to change. They may be contributing factors

that complicate your recovery or may need to be addressed sep-
arately. To modify or unlearn what may be deeply implanted in
you can be a challenge in itself and should not be underestimated.

> *"Healing doesn't mean the damage never existed.*
> *It means the damage no longer controls your life."*
> Akshay Dubey, journalist, writer

Controlling Disease

During an experience with a disease, we usually ask these common and sometimes baffling questions:

Where did it come from?   How did I get it?
Could I have prevented it?   How bad is it?

When we ask these questions, you basically are attempting to understand how much control you had in getting it, dealing with it, and preventing it.

Most humans want or need to have some level of control over their lives. No matter how hard you try, some things are outside your control. You have done everything right; you just did not stop it, reduce it, or prevent it. The outcome simply did not turn out as anticipated. This section of the book will attempt to help you understand some important related concepts.

Let us distinguish among several terms which you have already and will continue to encounter in the latter part of this book. They have been modified slightly from their medical usage.

Treating is the process of attempting to fix any disease or injury.

Healing refers to damage, wounds, or injuries which are in the process of getting better or going away.

Curing means to eliminate the disease entirely.

Recovery is focused on the return to normal functioning or a former state.

Development is the opportunity to learn, nurture, or advance a skill or ability you may have never had.

Notes:

- You can **treat** a disease, but that does not mean the person will be **cured** or **healed**.
- There are many steps involved in **recovery**, and **healing** is the first of these steps.

Infection

At some point you may ask yourself, where did this disease come from? As presented in the opening of the book, all leaders will encounter and contract leadership diseases during their time in leadership positions. It is inevitable. Although it may be quite interesting to analyze the origins of a disease and the reasons why you contracted it, it is most important to simply recognize when you are leadersick.

As you heal and recover, you may want to consider how to prevent it from happening again. At that time, the questions of how and why you got it become more relevant. As you begin your analysis, recognize there are internal and external factors. Both play a role, often in a complex integration. Determining the balance between the two, may help your understanding. Having a better grasp of the infection process will aid in earlier detection and a quicker implementation of treatment in the future.

Consider that you may have a propensity toward self-contamination by placing yourself in circumstances and conditions where you are exposed to certain diseases. You might easily be coerced or find it difficult to refuse undesirable or risky situations. There may even be times when you can do little or nothing to prevent or avoid exposure. Sometimes it is involuntary exposure, but other times it may be willful negligence.

Some of you may want to compare how certain personal characteristics and behaviors align with symptoms common to specific diseases. How do your strengths and weaknesses intersect with it? How are certain types of personalities drawn toward one type of disease? How do your common actions and habits make you predisposed to a particular disease?

You may also find yourself contaminated by a toxic culture or dysfunctional organization where symptoms are considered acceptable or are routinely ignored. Being leadersick may be the norm. Some of you will find yourself in a subordinate position with another leader or working for a boss who firmly demands or gently recommends you believe or think in a certain way. You may be told or asked to say or do something which may expose you to a higher risk of a certain disease.

If a role model or mentor has one or more of the diseases, it may be difficult for you to recognize those diseases and how they may impact you. If there is a leader you highly admire, it may nearly be impossible for you to believe that person has any diseases. You may overlook them intentionally or subconsciously.

For younger or newer leaders and those who have only experienced poor or toxic leadership, you may not know what good or great leadership looks like and find yourself emulating someone who is leadersick or even toxic. Assess them by using this book and see what you discover.

Obviously, if you spend a significant amount of time around those who have already contracted a disease, there is a higher probability of contracting it. It may become a bigger problem if you have contracted one and do not tell anyone or continually deny it. At any rate, you run the risk of infecting others.

As you analyze, take a look at diseases which have similarities or are affiliated with another one. You may be prone to catching a specific one or be predisposed to contract one. Probabilities of catching something vary dramatically from person to person.

Doctors have told me there are people who use their illness and/or its treatment as part of their identity; in other words, it defines who they are and getting well could cost them their identity. That would be an interesting dilemma for a person wanting to be rid of a disease.

Severity

You may have noticed that this book did not deal with extreme cases where there is repetitive lying, outright cheating, extreme manipulation, aggressive actions, or violent behavior. It is not about sociopathic behavior. I also avoided illegal activity and blatant ethical violations. These may exist and are more directly addressed in a later section entitled, Some People May Not Recover.

In the medical field, many diseases are measured or classified by levels of intensity, rating scales, or stages of development. With leadership diseases we work with levels of severity similar to the rating system for cancer.

Leadership Disease Stages

0 – None, Negligible

1 – Mild, Minor, Minimal

2 – Moderate, Significant,

3 – Serious, Advanced

4 – Extreme, Severe, Dangerous

If you reach 4, you can create your own definition or description. If you do not, others will, and their descriptions may be quite derogatory, unflattering, or harsh. No matter what words are used, at level 4, you are in deep trouble.

If a disease progresses rapidly, is not checked, or reaches the end of stage 3 and moves immediately into stage 4, there may be serious consequences for you and those you lead. A disease can leave people and an organization in complete disarray or in total collapse. When it is this serious, there can be workplace violence, sabotage, character assassination, or legal actions.

Another method for gauging severity would be a **pain assessment scale**. When you visit a medical facility, you are often asked your pain level on a scale of 1-10 with 10 being the most severe form of pain. A similar method may prove quite useful in determining which disease or what aspects of a disease is creating your greatest discomfort.

Such a rating system would help in setting priorities or determining the focus for assessment or treatment. You may want to concentrate on what is most painful to reduce its negative impact on your leadership and limit its distraction. On the flip side, you may want to handle one or a few lower-level pains to get them under control and allow you to invest your time and energy in dealing with the one which is greater. Knowing that most leaders will be experience more than one disease at a time, pain assessment may be a very helpful too.

Some of you who are deeply analytical may want to develop your own system with weighted measures, scaling, rankings, or any other system you know or have developed. If it works for you and helps in your diagnosis, use it.

Prevention

One of the common questions associated with prevention would be "Is there a vaccine for what ails me?" Sadly, and confidently, I can say no. The best practice is to follow the advice offered in the beginning of the book where we talked about the Formula for Leadership Health. It was a call to practice trust, honesty, and integrity. We expand on the equation a little further in the book in a later section called Maintaining Good Leadership Health.

Variations of that charge might include "Be trustworthy, honest, and a person of integrity" or "Build trust, practice honesty, and maintain integrity." We could classify these admonitions as ways for taking care of yourself and keeping a healthy leadership lifestyle. Adherence to this advice would not necessarily protect you from acquiring one disease or more, but it can make recovery shorter, easier, and more effective.

You also might ask, what can I do if exposed and have not caught it yet? Referring again to healthcare professionals' advice, it may be obvious to get away from the source of exposure. Observe what is being done by an infected leader and refrain from doing the same. If you become aware of an imminent disease, quickly take actions to reduce or control the impact.

When you are aware of your tendency to contract certain types of diseases or ones which share common symptoms, you can either create a prevention plan or you can wait and simply succumb. The simplest approach may be to observe what is being done by an infected leader and refrain from doing the same.

GETTING HELP

As a leader, seeking and getting feedback, encouragement, support, and advice from people you trust has been a theme in nearly every Treatment checklist section of the 28 diseases. Those repeated messages should have conveyed the importance of these modalities. Strong leaders have access to coaching and counseling built into their leadership regimen. It is part of adopting that age-old adage: Surround yourself with good (great) people.

Leaders frequently find themselves in need of a higher level of assistance, a more neutral party, or a method for digging deeper into their minds and hearts. They need to access opportunities to learn from those who have dealt with diseases in the past. At these times, coaches, counselors, therapists, mentors, and advisors can be immensely helpful.

Some leaders choose to engage in a relationship with someone who becomes a mentor. Mentors help leaders navigate through challenges where they often have familiarity and experience, or even expertise. There can be spiritual advisors such as pastors, clergy, or faith leaders who are focused on a leader's heart, soul, and spirit or faith, beliefs, and ideology. Some leaders enlist the help of trusted family members, close friends, or associates.

Sometimes resources are apparent and readily available. At other times they are difficult to find and scarce. Some organizations provide help for their leaders, but more often do not. Most of the time, you are on your own and must be diligent in locating, pursuing, and securing the help you may need.

Professional Coaching & Counseling

The use of professionals for coaching and counseling has gained traction over time, and the stigma associated with such has been reduced. Yet many leaders are reluctant and may even refuse to engage with someone in a coaching or counseling role.

There are significant benefits to having the assistance of a professional coach or counselor. These individuals can help leaders assess symptoms and reach a diagnosis of their leadership diseases. It is easy and common for leaders to overlook or not understand what is occurring in their leadership life. An observer can be more objective and have less bias. These individuals may also come to the table with demonstrated expertise and experience in serving in these roles.

Coaches usually fall into two categories:

1. Executive Coaches who primarily focus on professional or managerial roles (often connected to employment, job, or vocation)
2. Life Coaches who take a more wholistic approach toward a greater balance among all aspects of a leader's life and world.

A counselor or therapist is another route. These professionals focus on your mind, emotions, and behaviors. They strive to find the root causes and seek to help a person adjust, handle, and improve how they deal with personal issues and relationships. Obviously, such a person could be of great assistance to one who wants to lead better with a healthier psycho-social self.

Overcoming Your Reluctance

Some leaders are reluctant to engage another person in a helping role. Leaders often believe they do not or should not need help. They are used to being the helper or giver in relationships with others. They believe a leader is to be the strongest, less susceptible to the influence of human frailties. And needed help may be viewed as a weakness by others.

A leader needs to explore the **why** of reluctance. A leader may need encouragement, a referral, or even a hard push to seek guidance and advice. It is important for a leader to understand how and why highly successful leaders rely upon helping, supporting, and coaching relationships.

It is important to be reminded that taking care of yourself is essential to being a healthy leader. "You can't take care of others if you can't take care of yourself" is often quoted when we witness a leader who is unable to offer support, encouragement, and guidance to others. **Self-care** is not a bad concept. It asserts that keeping yourself in top condition and form will provide the energy, confidence, and clear thinking needed for doing your best.

Leaders who choose to incorporate helpers and guides within their lives usually become stronger and more effective. It is so important to have people in your life who are wise and discerning and who understand you, your dreams, your challenges, and your fears. Have someone who firmly holds you accountable for your progress, learning, and outcomes. Perhaps most important, have a person who will help you process your losses, pain, and failure, as well as your victories and triumphs.

The Healing Process

One definition of **healing** is "the process of making or becoming sound and healthy again" (lexico.com). This should be your goal in treating a disease. It can be a long process or a short one. It may be intense or mild. Much depends on the severity of your disease, the treatment steps you choose, and perhaps most importantly, your commitment to getting better. You will also need to determine if you are trying to manage it or overcome it.

Recognition and acceptance are the first steps and may be the most important parts of healing. They are essential. You cannot heal without admitting you have a disease and defining how severe it is. Once leaders realize and acknowledge a disease, they can select one or more strategies or treatments for healing.

One path is understanding the disease. The goal on this route is to gain a greater grasp of how you contracted it and how it is affecting you. This path is filled with questions. Where did it come from? How long have I had this? Why didn't I notice it? Why didn't someone tell me? How did I contribute to the disease? How has this malady impacted my leadership? You will find yourself looking for answers. Some of us are just curious. Others want to know in order to avoid it or better handle it in the future. Most of us want to understand the disease as part of our recovery.

The other path is treatment. It too is filled with questions, but those primarily focus on action. The answers to your questions help shape your treatment. What is my path to recovery? What are my treatment options? How much effort will it take? Who can I ask to help me?

As the Treatment checklist section of each disease demonstrates, there are many choices. Some will work for you, and others will not. Some treatment options may not be in the checklists. Other ideas may be your creation or may derive from another source. Bottom line, you need to discover and apply that which will help you heal.

For some leaders the issue of faith becomes part of their recovery process. A leader might be heard to say: "I could not have made it through this without my faith," "God stepped in and did what I could not," or "My healing came from a power beyond me." Occasionally, a leader's comment might be, "The worst thing leaders can do is to not trust God with their leadership." For some leaders, faith and prayer are an essential part of their healing.

Note: It is important to respect the treatment decisions and healing processes of others.

"Healing is a matter of time, but it is sometimes also a matter of opportunity."
Hippocrates

Helping Others Recover

Helping others to develop and expand their abilities is a very important aspect of highly effective leadership. Leaders build leaders. Knowing this, you should want to assist others in their battles with leadership diseases. Sometimes we are asked to help. Sometimes we just offer. And there are times when we need to intervene.

The way we enter a helping relationship is critical. When and how do you approach it? Are you the right person? What should you say or do? What is your role: information, guidance, or support? You may need to give another leader permission to set aside time, support to face the challenges, encouragement to take risks, tools to facilitate learning, and/or advice on treatment choices.

It is usually best to allow people to self-discover and make personal decisions, but there are times when you may need to be more direct. There is a much higher level of success when leaders acknowledge their diseases, create treatment plans, and implement them. Hopefully, a leader should know when, how, and who to ask for help. That is not always the case.

A critical part of helping another leader is to understand your role, and the types and styles of leadership employed by other leaders. Most leaders have a natural desire to be in charge. They struggle with whether to empower people or just do it for them. It is not easy to guide, coach, or support another leader. It is much simpler to tell them what to do. Many of us want to fix the person or the situation. Yet, we must recognize and address this desire to take charge.

Most of us realize that change and improvement have a higher success rate when people are invested in the actions which need to be taken. We call that *buy-in*. Your best approach might be guided questions of What do you think you should do? or What are your plans or next steps? Helping other leaders to consider options, create criteria, and evaluate alternatives can be of great assistance. The decisions they make and the actions they take, coupled with your encouragement and support, make a powerful combination.

Yet there are times when leaders are so stuck or dramatically leadersick that they cannot think clearly, make good decisions, or implement any actions. A firm directive might be needed. Many of us have heard the medical professional say, "You must take this medicine every day," or "Follow the treatment regimen I prescribed." Those commands are often followed with a harsh reminder of a harsh consequence. "And if you don't, it will get worse, you will never recover, or (the worse statement) you will die."

Understanding the value of being a *helper* rather than a *doer* may make this task easier. Imparting your knowledge and experience gives you time to think about what you have done to combat diseases. This will generate new perspectives for you while helping others learn. Helping others heal can be a part of your own healing.

As with other common physical and mental illnesses, you can choose to distance yourself from those infected so as not to catch anything or so you can pity those who are already leadersick. The alternative is to help others work toward recovery. It is not an easy task, but that is what good leaders do.

> *"As soon as healing takes place, go out and heal somebody else."*
> Maya Angelou, memoirist, poet, activist

MAINTAINING GOOD LEADERSHIP HEALTH

In the earlier portion of the book, you were introduced to a formula similar to the health adage of "Eat right, exercise, and get plenty of rest." You were offered a modified version specifically for leaders: *Have integrity, be honest, and build trust.* You were promised that we would expand upon these three qualities later in the book.

A tremendous amount of research and literature has been devoted to the importance of these three virtues. They have been debated, dissected, and analyzed in nearly every way possible. Current culture, environment, and climate play an important role as groups and individuals present and defend their perspectives.

The important question for each of us to struggle with is this: What does it mean to have them in your life, or what happens when they are absent? We wanted to shed a little light on the three as they relate to leadership diseases. We hope it will reinforce the need to not only know this mantra but practice it every day of your leadership life.

INTEGRITY + HONESTY + TRUST = HEALTHIER LEADERSHIP

Integrity

This value is most often defined as a firm adherence to a code or standard of morals or values, an uprightness or incorruptibility of character or action (merriam-webster.com). Words such as decency, goodness, and virtue of often used to describe integrity.

Lack of integrity can be perceived in many ways. Here are some of the most obvious, but there can be others:

- Cheating
- Stealing
- Lying
- Exploitation

- Illegal Activities
- Procedural Disregard
- Ethics Violations
- Policy Rejection
- Undeserved Acceptance of Credit

A crisis of integrity may result in a leader's being viewed as dishonest, fearful, a failure, a fraud, and insecure. When you lack integrity, it impacts every aspect of your leadership life. A lack of integrity is often correlated with a lack of moral or ethical values.

Leaders need to know they are being watched all the time for the smallest indication that they are not walking the talk. Leaders cannot be *Do as I say not as I do*. People are always watching to see if they are true to their expressed values. Every decision that is made and the actions you take must have integrity and *doing the right thing* as their foundation.

Much has been written on this subject of integrity. As it relates to disease, a few helpful tips are included here. Control your negative emotions and make decisions for the good of others. You may want to convey that it was not your intention to do, say, or believe something that led to your affliction.

The bottom line is that it's about integrity and authenticity. Understand who you are and what you stand for, behave in a manner that is consistent with your words, values, and beliefs. Treat others fairly, and work to include all voices. Fulfill your commitments.

Honesty

Healthy leaders are honest. Drawing from several perspectives, honest is defined as free of deceit and untruthfulness, sincere, morally correct, or virtuous. Good leaders care about honesty and truth. The two are so interwoven, it is difficult to talk about one without the other. Most of us want to follow a leader who we view as honest and truthful. It is about perception. If the leader is not honest, the leader loses, but so does the organization and its efforts.

A compound definition of truth is, defined as a fact or belief that is accepted as true, or that which is true or in accordance with fact or reality. Here is where it gets tricky and may sound as though you are enrolled in a philosophy class. What is truth? What is fact? What is reality? Most of us have heard two opposite statements, and both were presented as the truth. Two people can review the same information and arrive at a very different conclusion, both believing theirs to be reality.

Dishonesty appears in many forms: not being candid, distorting or disputing what others believe to be factual, or making promises and not delivering on them. People may view changing your mind as a form of dishonesty. You might say something to be funny, but it is perceived as an untruth. When you try to please or appease others, some may see this as a way of being dishonest.

When a leader is perceived as dishonest, there are many repercussions. People question what you are telling them, or they stop believing anything you say. It can elevate to a point where others are absolutely certain what you are saying is a lie. Even when you attempt to be honest, they may not believe it and cannot rely on you for needed information.

Dishonesty can be when you do not correct what you know to be a lie, or you tolerate what it does to you, others, or the organization. Some leaders may have a very difficult time recognizing or believing the truth. They are confused by reality and end up refusing facts and rejecting the truth.

Dishonesty also has a direct negative connection to trust and integrity. If people believe you are lying, they will not trust you. It is often said that it will eventually catch up with you, meaning that when people figure it out or change their mind about you, there are serious consequences.

If leaders are not honest with themselves or others, how can they expect their people to be honest? If leaders are not honest, it can lead organizational fear, failure, and fraud. It can manifest itself through misreporting, poor strategies, financial loss, and might even rise to the level of criminal activity.

The problem can get worse when the leader will not acknowledge a perception of dishonesty. If you are viewed as dishonest, you will no longer be able to effectively lead, or will no longer be thought of as a leader.

Trust

Trust seems to be a less complex principle than honesty and integrity. The definition has fewer nuances or interpretations. When people have a firm belief in the reliability, truth, ability, and strength of their leaders, there is trust. It is still a matter of perception.

Effective leadership is built on trust, which leads to positive relationships with those within and without, below and above. Failing to follow through on promises or behaving in a manner that contradicts your words creates a lack of trust on a personal level. If you are considered untrustworthy, all matters which deal with goals, direction, instructions, and information are suspect or ineffective.

Trust is also an issue of reciprocity. If leaders are to be trusted, they must trust. Why should or would we trust someone who does not trust us? Trust is earned by both parties. Many of us trust quickly and wholly. We believe in a concept of *I will trust you until you break that trust.* It does not work that way with everyone. Leaders and their people must build and nurture trust. It is tested and challenged. If it is broken, repair is incredibly difficult, and in some instances, impossible to regain.

If you have very low or no credibility, lack integrity, or are dishonest, there will be little or no trust in you as a leader. Lacking one of these three puts your leadership in jeopardy. If two are missing, your condition is critical. If you are deficit in all three, your leadership is terminal.

RELATED ISSUES

Communication Is Vital

You probably noticed that the inability to communicate or poor communication were not classified as specific diseases. Communication can be compared to proper circulation of the blood in your body. Without flowing properly, you will have a serious problem. Blood absorbs oxygen from air in the lungs, removes carbon dioxide, provides oxygen to cells, transports nutrients to the body, forms blood clots to prevent blood loss, and carries antibodies which fight infection.

Communication has similar functions. It absorbs what is said and done, removes obstacles, provides clarity, and transports information. It needs to happen effectively, efficiently, and regularly. Communication is intertwined with every aspect of good leadership. When it does not work properly, healing, treatment, recovery, and prevention occur much more slowly and with fewer enduring outcomes.

Some might say it is better to over-communicate than do the opposite. Remember, communication includes good listening. Under-communication may foster negative consequences through faulty assumptions, unclear motives, misunderstood rationales, and inadequate strategies. Restricted blood flow is not good. Ample movement of communication, like that of your life fluid, creates better outcomes.

In terms of being leadersick, leaders must make a commitment to communicate what is going on within themselves, how a disease is impacting them and others, plus what needs to be done to address it. Since communication is inherent to almost every aspect of leadership, it must be an essential and vital focus for any leader. Leaders must consistently communicate using all appropriate methods possible.

It is crippling if you cannot communicate clearly and understandably. Yet, you do not have to be a great communicator to be a healthy leader. However, you have to be seen as someone who has recognized that weakness and is trying to overcome it by utilizing others for support and assistance, while even at times, letting others do it for you.

With most health concerns a blood screening is conducted to provide important information for understanding a patient's illness or condition. Similar to the blood test, reviewing and analyzing a leader's communication will tell us much about how well it is working and what may be wrong.

People Are Complex

Much of this book builds upon the fragile and vital relationships between people: leader to colleague, leader to employee, leader to team, leader to boss, leader to student, leader to members, leader to leader. From the brain, eyes, ears, subconscious, soul, heart, and bodies of relational people, we draw and receive feedback, support, assistance, information, opinions, suggestions, ideas, observations, and more.

These people are a complex collection of what they came into this world with and what they have experienced while here. Figuring out **what** people are feeling, thinking, or believing is difficult enough, unless they come right out and tell you. Even then, their true feelings may be cloaked in misperceptions, insecurities, and false impressions about how the world around them works.

Figuring out **why** people think and act as they do is even more difficult. Leaders should consciously acknowledge and remind themselves that people are different and likely come from backgrounds entirely alien to that which we have experienced. There are reasons why people think and behave as they do. Attempt to discover what these might be so you can avoid making assumptions about others based purely on their behavior.

On the other hand, when others come to you with information, be objective about what you hear and try not to render either support for it or a judgment concerning it. If it was offered openly and sincerely, as far as you can tell, accept it, and thank them for sharing. If the information was feedback for you on your leadership – difficult to obtain unless actively sought by you – pay very close attention to it. They are likely sticking their neck out a bit to offer their thoughts; respect that fact and even acknowledge it to them.

Impact of Fear

Fear is a powerful and hidden emotional handicap in nearly every disease. If you are afraid, it becomes more difficult to recognize, understand, and treat your affliction. What is the fear? Is it not being able to admit you are leadersick? Is it facing the impact it has or could have on you? Is it wasting time and effort to address the disease? Is it simply fear of the unknown?

Fear can produce deep concern over issues which are very important to leaders, such as loss of trust and credibility. There may be worries about the damage done to a leader's prestige, finances, power, and reputation. These fears can make a leader appear weak, indecisive, and incompetent. Few want to follow leaders who seem to have lost confidence, vision, and/or clarity.

Fears can restrict leaders from meeting the needs of staff, volunteers, and the overall organization. It can cause leaders to not delegate, withhold important information, restrict planning, and withdraw when leadership is badly needed. When fear has a firm hold, one can be blinded to the importance of needed changes, a plan to move forward, or letting go of the past. Fear can cripple or destroy your ability to address your leadership diseases.

Fear is a natural condition and is part of the human experience. Leaders often feel they must rise above an emotion like fear. We hear in our heads, "Always be confident, never let them see you sweat, be decisive, never show fear." These admonitions can be harmful. People want to follow a leader who emanates humanity and authenticity.

As a leader, you need to explore your fears. Do not allow them to hold you back. It is not an easy task but one that is vital and significantly enhanced through intervention, wisdom, and support of an outside person. The utilization of a coach, mentor, therapist, or trusted advisor can help you discover and face your fears. Take the steps to find and engage such a person, or perhaps even more than one.

Being a Role Model

A leader needs to be healthy as a role model. Being sick all the time or not treating your diseases sends a signal to your people that it's OK to show up with your active symptoms, spreading them to anyone and everyone.

Not leading by example gives a false impression that it is OK to talk the talk and not walk the walk. True leaders would not ask someone to do anything they would not do themselves. Sometimes showing your strengths, talents, and skills will help solidify *buy-in* and build a collaborative relationship. Not leading by example sets a negative tone that does not drive results.

Some People May Not Recover

Some leaders will never admit they have or have had even one disease. Others will recognize they have one or more but refuse treatment. Then, there are leaders for whom treatment has failed. Their attempt was crippled by an unwillingness to act or a lack of commitment. Finally, although it may be a miniscule group, there are leaders who are not treatable. Even if they wanted to deal with their illnesses, they are damaged so severely, it would take a miracle to recover.

Leaders who have contracted multiple diseases and left them unchecked for many years will find themselves in an incredibly difficult situation. Refusal to face the reality of their diseases or a complete neglect can lead to crippling circumstances. It may also occur through involvement in major or multiple ethical violations, illegal activities, or loss of moral compass. When a leader's condition has reached these high levels of severity, restoration is nearly impossible.

Upon reaching such a point, a leader's credibility and reputation are damaged severely. Both of those attributes are fragile. They take years, even decades, to build, and yet one incident can destroy them. When this occurs, a leader has clearly validated to others a lack of integrity, a lack of honesty, and a lack of trust. Without those three requisites of good leadership health, such a person is in a desperate situation.

If the diseases have advanced to an extreme level, an attempt to recover will be a painful process, often with little hope of success. Most leaders are unwilling to make such an effort or face the odds. A person who attempts to return to any level of leadership must realize it is a long and difficult road back. A leader will have great difficulty in finding those who will give support, intervene when needed, or oversee a complex treatment regimen.

Some might say that the best approach may be to get a fresh start. In some situations, it might work. Although it may be expensive, there are people and services which can be accessed if a former leader is willing to pay. If a fall from leadership has occurred before and there was a successful return to former prominence, it may require a tremendous effort to make it happen again. It is even a greater challenge if the leader has made a comeback more than once.

Shakespeare said, "The evil that men do lives after them; the good is oft interred with their bones." Human beings tend to remember the bad about others more than the good. That is why it is said, "Some may not recover."

Be a Healthy Leader

Every leader should want to be at top form, healthy, and ready to face the challenges. When we are healthy leaders and not burdened, restricted, and/or damaged by leadership diseases, we can be at our best. No one wants to be *leadersick*; it feels lousy.

A leader needs to strive to be a healthy leader. Yes, a healthy mind, body, and spirit are very important, but leadership health is important, too. Remind yourself, no matter what you have now, you can get better. By reading and applying this book, you have taken the first step, if not several important steps, toward becoming a better leader.

When someone is or has been sick, we ask, "How are you feeling?" You often hear the typical responses of "I'm good", "I'm doing alright" or "I'm getting better!" Good leaders are usually in a continual state of change: growing and improving or shrinking and declining. This means, in terms of our leadership health, we are usually getting better or getting worse.

Yes, there is always the choice of bumbling along in life with middle-of-the-road health. Leadership health can be the same. You can just do what's adequate, be average, or do a fair job, and you probably will not suffer much. But you will not be the admired and respected *picture of leadership health*.

Make the choice to get better and improve your leadership health. You can do it, and so can all leaders who make the pledge and commitment to be healthier. Remember, also, that it is about helping other leaders become healthier and better. Because we all know, **when leaders get better, we all get better.**

WHAT'S NEXT

There is so much more that could have been added to this book. As we went to print, additional ideas and perspectives kept coming from my early readers and reviewers. We knew this book would not be all inclusive and cover every aspect of these leadership diseases completely.

It has been our hope that you would be stimulated or challenged to think in a different way about your leadership or the leadership of others. We knew that some of you would uncover additional symptoms and impacts. We hope that you would discover new treatment ideas or create your own.

Leadersick has been a journey, much like the journey of every leader. We hope it has enhanced your navigation and provided new paths to explore. If this book has intrigued you, opened new possibilities, and caused you to change now slightly or dramatically you practiced your leadership, we have done our job.

 We want to hear from you and interact through our website LeadersickBook.com. Take a look and become part of the healing community of dynamic leaders who are accepting the challenge of **Becoming a Healthy Leader.**

ACKNOWLEDGMENTS

Please do not ignore the sizeable cast who have contributed to this book. Many people will scan through the credits at the end of a movie failing to appreciate all who made the film. There were 94 individuals who became part of my Leadersick Team and deserve to be recognized for what they have brought to this project. It was not just the efforts of the author, but a collaboration of highly successful leaders who offered their time and wisdom.

Special Thanks

Mike Baird was my sounding board, proofreader, idea generator, protagonist, and analyst. He was my go-to guy for any issue pertaining to the book. Mike supported this project from start to finish and had a profound impact on its content.

Ric Keaster painstakingly edited the manuscript, provided fresh ideas, and offered improved word choices, better phrases, and brought life to the disease names. He taught me more about the English language and writing than any teacher I have ever had.

Troy Linker is an incredible layout editor. He tolerated my strong opinions and truly valued my input. His knowledge and navigation skills in publishing were invaluable. He gave me so much more than I could have ever expected.

Rick Kirkpatrick used his creative skills and ingenious mind to painstakingly produce the graphics and artwork for the book. I was thrilled to have his good humor and collaboration as my brother. It was way better than when we shared a room as kids.

Leadersick Team

As mentioned, several times, the pages of this book are filled with the thoughts, ideas, and lessons learned from seasoned leaders. Being part of the Leadersick Team does not mean they ARE leadersick. Instead, it says that they are leaders who have been through the ailments, illnesses, and anguish which all leaders experience. The difference is, their success at self-diagnosis, treatment, healing, and recovery existed long before this book was ever written.

There is no simple way to recognize what each has accomplished in his or her leadership lives. A list of all those who have contributed is now provided followed by a compilation of their backgrounds and affiliations as a whole.

CONTRIBUTOR BACKGROUNDS & CREDENTIALS

It was challenging to present the substantial and significant backgrounds and credentials of the 94 amazing leaders who contributed to this book. All of them have held multiple titles, served in a variety of roles, and were engaged in numerous places. Rather than list each by name with accompanying references, we wanted to provide a collective picture of the entire group demonstrating the vast and diverse set of experience from which they came.

Contributors

Tehseen Ali Kazmi, Tony Alter, Alena Anisimava, Debbie Anselm, J. Michael Baird, Allyson Baughman, Nancy Baumann, Calvin Bellamy, Jená Bellezza, Michael J. Berta Jr., Lizbeth A. Bryant, Peggy Buffington, Sergey Bulavsky, John Cain, Dorothy Ige Campbell, Kitty Campbell, Gerald Chabot, Ed Charbonnau, Abir Clark, Elias Crim, John H. Davies, Frances Desmond, Angie Nelson Deuitch, Matthew W. Deulley, Lincoln D. Ellis, Otukeyi Emmanuel, Lorri Feldt, Gina Fezler, James W. Flannery, Karen M. Freeman-Wilson, Vincent Galbiati, Ali Ghalayini, Donna Golob, Michael W. Griffin, Moises Guadron, Arjun Gupta, Danielle Harris, Colleen Hickman, David C. Hill, Juliann Jankowski, Jim Jessup, Jim Jorgensen, Ric Keaster, James Kirkpatrick, Richard Kirkpatrick, Nathan H. Kleefisch, Andrew S. Kyres, Danny Lackey,

Dyke E. Lee, Sr., Donald Lesch, Troy Linker, Rudy López, Daniel Lowery, George D. Lundberg, Patricia Lorimer Lundberg, Mark Maassel, Natalia Makayeva, Irena Mamonova, Gregory Mance, Meghan Manilla, Vanessa Allen McCloud, Stewart McMillan, Joan McPherson, Jim McShane, Blair Milo, Robyn Minton-Holmes, Pamela Mishler-Fish, Leigh Morris, Randy Niemeyer, Uzoma F. Obidike, Kim Olesker, Robert Ordway, Audra Peterson, Leslie Plesac, Rick Riddering, Cynthia Roberts, Paul J. Schlottman, Max Schlueter, Edward Schoenfelt, Michelle M. Searer, Aco Sikoski, Violet Sistovaris, Maggi Spartz, Ryan Straney, Bowdeya Tweh, Theresa Valade, Steve A. Varela, Frances Vega-Steele, Kris J. Vos, Chelsea L. Whittington, Denise E. Williams, Linda Woloshansky, Yan Yang, Gail Zurek.

Age Groups

< 30	1%
30s	7%
40s	12%
50s	26%
60s	29%
70s	22%
80+	3%

Gender

Male 53% Female 47%

Highest Level of Education

Some College or High School	2%
Undergraduate Degree	23%
Masters/Postgraduate	45%
Doctorate	30%

Ethnic, Family or Cultural Background
(multiple choices could be selected)

Western Europe 59%

Eastern Europe 22%

Latin/South America 8%

Africa 15%

Asia/Pacific Region 3%

Middle East/India 6%

Native/Indigenous 7%

Primary Fields and Sectors of Employment
(multiple choices could be selected)

Communications/Media 21%

Community Organization 37%

Construction/Real Estate/Energy 8%

Economic/Workforce Development 15%

Finance/Accounting/Business Services 26%

Government 25%

Healthcare 14%

Higher Education 41%

Human/Social Services 20%

Information Technology 11%

K-12/Early Childhood Education 20%

Legal/Law Enforcement 10%

Recreation/Leisure/Arts 9%

Religious/Faith based 15%

Retail/Consumer Services 13%

Transportation/Distribution/Logistics 5%

Wholesale/Industrial/Manufacturing 14%

Human/Social Services 20%

Prominent or Primary Titles Held in Work Settings

Multiple answers were consolidated to avoid repetition and abbreviate the list (each could provide three).

Adjunct Professor, Area Manager, Assistant Manager, Assistant Project Manager, Assistant Superintendent, Assistant Vice Chancellor, Associate Dean, Associate Director, Associate Professor, Associate Vice Chancellor, Attorney General, Brand Strategist, Business Growth Strategist, Campaign Manager, Career Transition Coach, Chair, Chairman, Chancellor, Chaplain, Chief Executive Officer, Chief Information Officer, Chief of Police, Chief Operating Officer, Clerk-Treasurer, Coach, Community Organizer, Coordinator, Copywriter, Council President, County Clerk, Dean, Department Chair, Deputy Bureau Chief, Deputy Commissioner, Design Director, Detective, Development Director, Director, Director of Career & Technical Education, Director of Diversity & Student Support, Director of External Affairs & Special Events, Director of Marketing & Communications, Director of Operations & School Safety, Director of Out-client Services, Director of Products, Director of Sales & Marketing, Director of Student Development, Director of Technology, Director of Warehousing & Logistics, Director-Quality Assurance, Director-Congregation & Community Relations, Director-New Business Development & Finance, Directory of Marketing & Promotions, District Manager, Editor, Editor in Chief, Engineer, Executive Director, Executive General Counsel, Executive Vice President & Chief Experience Officer, Finance Director, Founder, Founding Managing Director, General Manager, Group Leader, HS Principal, Leadership Consultant, Lieutenant Commander, Manager, Managing Director, Marketing Manager, Mayor, Medical Director, Music Director,

Operations Manager, Owner, Partner, Pastor, Plant Manager, President, President/CEO, Principal, Partner, Professor, Program Chair, Program Director, Program Manager, Project Coordinator, Project Manager, Publisher, Regional Director, Regional President, School Superintendent, Secretary of Career Connections & Talent, Senior Consultant, Senior Director, Senior Examiner, Senior Manager, Senior Pastor, Senior Vice President, Site Director, Software Engineer, State Director, State Senator, Superintendent, Superintendent of Schools, Supervisor, Task Force Commander, Teacher, Team Leader, Treasury Analyst, Vice Chairman, Vice Chancellor, Vice President, VP Business Development.

Primary or Prominent Organizational Affiliations in Paid Position

Multiple answers were given for some affiliations but listed only once. Some names were shortened or reduced to the brand or recognized name. Most geographic references were dropped since many respondents worked in same or similar organizations in various locations (each could provide up to four).

Private Sector

Accenture, Aldi, Alverno Labs, ArcelorMittal, AT&T, BelHard, BMO Harris, Brightway Wealth Management, Chicago Board of Trade, Chicago Tribune, Community Healthcare System, Cureus, Dow Jones, Facebook, FGM Architects, First Financial Bank, Gannett, General Mills, Genuine Parts Company, Gough & Lesch Development, Hallmark, Health Management Associates, Hill Construction, Hoeppner Wagner & Evans, Indiana Federal Bank, International Harvester, Johnson Publishing, Kiss Technologies, Krieg DeVault, Kyriba, La Porte Hospital, Lee Enterprises, Linker Publishing, Litho Press, Magro Construction, McColly Real Estate, Mead/ACCO, MMS, Motorola, Motto, Niemeyer Milk, NIPSCO, Northern Trust, Northwestern Mutual, Odyssey Restaurant, Peoples Bank, Pinnacle Banks, Quad City Times, Riverstone

Financial Advisors, Robert Half, Romma, She Leads Beautifully, Star Plaza Theatre, Tipalti Solutions, UPS, Wazir & Sons, Whirlpool, WNIT.

Education

Universities
Belarus State, California-San Francisco, City University of New York, Dayton, George Mason, Indiana, Metropolitan State, Northwestern, Norwich, Purdue, Southeastern Louisiana, Southern Illinois, Southern Mississippi, Stanford, Trinity Christian, Tunghai, Valparaiso, Vincennes, Western Kentucky.

Colleges
Calumet of St. Joseph, Crossroads Bible, Emirates College for Advanced Education, Ivy Tech Community College, South Suburban College, Edison Electric Institute, Indiana Institute of Technology, IPM Business School, McCormick Seminary.

Schools
Blackford County, Calvary Lutheran HS, Ferndale Public, Gary Community, Marceline RV, Merrillville Community, Boone Township, Penn Harris Madison, Porter Township, Hobart, South Bend Career & Success Academies, St. James R-1, Tri-Creek, Union Township, Valparaiso Community, Warsaw Community.

Public Sector
Association of Career and Technical Education, California Department of Justice, Center of Workforce Innovations, California School Boards Association, City of Gary, City of La Porte, City of Valparaiso, Crime Research Group, Crossroads Workforce Investment Board, Federal Deposit Insurance Corporation, Federal Reserve Bank, Griffith Police, Indiana Department of Transportation, Indiana Economic Development Corporation, Indiana Workforce Board Association, Indiana Chamber of Commerce, Indiana Energy Association, Leadership Lafayette, Major Crimes Task Force,

National Association of Drug Court Professionals, National League of Cities, NI Forum, Office of Career & Technical Education, Porter County Election Board, Small Business Development Center, Social Security Adminstration, Town of Cedar Lake, Town of Highland, U.S. Army, U.S. Conference of Mayors, U.S. Navy, U.S. Treasury, Vermont Crime Information Center, Visalia Chamber of Commerce, Western Association of Chamber Executives, Workforce Alliance.

Nonprofit/Community Services

Adoptions & Aid International, African American Leadership Partnership, Alzheimer's Association, American Bankers Association, American Cancer Society, American Library Association, American Society of Clinical Pathologists, Association of Business Administration, Boys & Girls Clubs, Caminos de Agua, Catholic Diocese, Center for Church Renewal, Center for Community Change, Chicago Urban League, Christian Reformed Churches, Community Action Council, Conference on College Composition & Communication, Crossroads Community Church, Custom Tailor & Designers Association, Domestic Violence Resource Center, Dunes Learning Center, Evangelical Covenant Church, Faith Church, First Tabernacle Baptist, Food Bank, Girl Scouts, Harbor Light Hospice, Home Field Advantage Foundation, Humanities West, Indiana Parenting Institute, Kirika Child Development Centre, Lake Area United Way, Lake County Agricultural Society, Laurel Ministries, Ministry of Economy of RB, National Communication Association, National Council of Teachers of English, National Rifle Association, Northwest Indiana Symphony Orchestra, Positive Approach to Teen Health, Quality of Life Council, Registry for Presidents, South Shore Arts, Sunlight Community Church, The Night Ministry, Tomorrow's Cures Today Foundation, U.S. Hispanic Leadership Institute, Unity Foundation, Visiting Nurses, Wellstone Action, Youth Service Bureau, YouthBuild, YWCA.

Prominent or Primary Titles Held in Voluntary Roles

Multiple answers were consolidated to avoid repetition and abbreviate the list (each could provide three).

Advisor, Alpine Patroller, Board Chair, Board Member, Board President, Board Secretary, Board Vice Chair, Build Leader, Cabinet Member, Campaign Chair, Chair, Chairman, Chairperson, Chairwoman, Chaperon, Chaplain, Chief, Club Manager, Club Secretary, Co-chair, Coach, Commissioner, Committee Chair, Communications Copyeditor, Communion Minister, Community Care Elder, Community Organizer, Coordinator, Council Member, Council President, Counselor, Deputy Chief, Director, Elder, Emergency Medical Responder, Emeritus, Events & Hospitality Chair, Executive Board Member, Facilitator, Fellow, Founder, Founding Member, Fundraising Chair, Grants Chair, Honorary Commander, Instructor, Liaison, Manager, Marketing & Outreach Chair, Mentor, Minister, National Vice President, Newsletter Editor, Outreach Director, Parliamentarian, President, Projects Coordinator, Radio & TV Host, Reading Mentor, Scholarship Coordinator, School Board Member, Scout Leader, Scoutmaster, Secretary, Secretary/Treasurer, Senior Advisor, Special Events Coordinator, Sunday School Teacher, Team Leader, Treasurer, Trustee, Vice Chairman, Vice President, Volunteer, Volunteer Coordinator, Volunteer Director.

Primary or Prominent Organizational Affiliations as a Volunteer

Multiple answers were given for some affiliations but listed only once. Some names were shortened or reduced to the brand or recognized name. Most geographic references were dropped since many respondents worked in same or similar organizations in various locations (each could provide up to four).

Affordable Housing Advisory, After School Network, Alliance of Youth Leaders, Alpha Kappa Alpha, Alpha Xi Delta, Alumni

Club, American Hospital Association, American Library
Association, American Marketing Association, American
Medical Association, Art Museum, Arts & Creative Dis-
trict, Arts Center, Arts Federation, Aspen Institute, Asso-
ciation of Chamber Executives, Association of Leadership
Programs, Banta Neighborhood Association, Bar Associa-
tion, Barbershop Harmony Society, Baseball Boosters, Boy
Scouts of America, Boys & Girls Clubs, Business Council
for International Understanding, Business League, Cancer
Commons, Cancer Survivor Network, Caring Place, CASA,
Catholic Charities, Center of Workforce Innovations, Central
Asian Productivity Research Center, Chamber of Commerce,
Children of Chernobyl, Children's Hospice, Choice Books,
Christian Counseling Center, Christian Fellowship Minis-
tries, Citizens Advisory, Civic Theatre, Community Action,
Community College, Community Foundation, Community
Outreach Program, Community Theater, Compassion Inter-
national, Conservation Association, Continuum of Care,
Council on Educational Administration, County Park Foun-
dation,County Prison, Crisis Center, Deaf Services, Delta
Sigma Theta, Discoveries Unlimited, Diversity Leadership
Initiative, Domestic Violence Commission, Economic Devel-
opment Corporation, Education Foundation, Everybody
Wins, Family Advocates, Family Services, First Responder
Training Center, Food Pantry, Fraternal Order of Police,
Friends of the National Library of Medicine, Friends of
Ukraine Adoption, Girl Scouts, Girls on the Run, Governors
Commission on Diversity, Greater Federation of Women's
Clubs, Habitat for Humanity, Health Centers, Helping Other
Women, Hijos de Borinquen, Historic Preservation, Hospice,
Hospital Board, Humane Society, Indiana Humanities, Influ-
ential Women Association, International Bullying Prevention
Association, Johnny Appleseed, Junior Achievement, Kappa
Kappa Kappa, Kiwanis, Leadership Foundation, League
of Municipal Clerks & Treasurers, Learning Center, Lions
Club, Little League, Lutheran Services, Meals on Wheels,
Memorial Theatre, Mental Health America, Metropolitan

Correctional Facility, NAACP, National Academy of Medicine, National Association of Women Business Owners, National Contract Management Association, National Council of Teachers, National Parenting Education Network, National Ski Patrol, National Writing Project, Neighborhood House, Performing Arts Center, Philanthropy Alliance, Planned Parenthood, Principals Association, Public Television, Rebuild Together, Red Cross, Regional Plan Commission, Regulated Amusement Device Board, Rotary, Savation Army, Second Chance, Shared Ethics Advisory, Small Business Development Center, Society of Innovators, State Senate, State Water Pollution Control Board, Substance Abuse Council, Suicide Prevention Council, Superintendents Association, Symphony Orchestra, Township Republicans, United States Hispanic Leadership Institute, United Way, Urban League, US Penitentiary, Wellstone Action, Wildlife Refuge, Women Business Development Center, World Trade Alliance, YMCA, Youth Employment Council, YWCA.

Countries, Cities & U.S. States
(lived for more than three years)

Countries
Australia, Belarus, Belize, Brazil, China, England, El Salvador, Greece, Hungary, India, Indonesia, Italy, Macedonia, Pakistan, Russia, Taiwan, Uganda, United Arab Emerites, Zimbabwe.

Cities
San Francisco, Austin, Beijing, Chicago, Cincinnati, Denver, Detroit, Indianapolis, Kansas City, Kolkata, Little Rock, London, Los Angeles, Memphis, Minneapolis, Minsk, Mumbai, New Orleans, New York, Omaha, Pittsburgh, Qingdao, Richmond, Rio de Janeiro, Tampa, Washington DC.

U.S. States
Alabama, Arkansas, California, Colorado, Florida, Georgia, Illinois, Indiana, Iowa, Kentucky, Louisiana, Massachusetts,

Michigan, Minnesota, Mississippi, Missouri, Nevada, New Hampshire, New Mexico, New York, Ohio, Pennsylvania, South Carolina, Tennessee, Texas, Vermont, Virginia, Washington, West Virginia, Wisconsin.

METHODOLOGY

Many of the readers may be curious about where and how the input was sought and utilized. While this effort does not technically qualify as qualitative research, it does employ some features of that established and scientific process. As mentioned previously, the Leadersick Team were engaged through discussion groups, interviews, video chats, and surveys. They were respondents, readers, and reviewers.

From a plethora of notes, transcripts, written responses, emails, and survey responses, I reviewed and sorted their ideas, answers, and thoughts into groups. It took many months to analyze, refine, and pare down the data.

From there, 18 people read portions of the manuscript at various times. Several others provided thoughts on specific sections of the book. Thirty-five people reviewed and proofed two to four disease chapters each. In the end, 15 dedicated individuals read the entire book prior to publication.

I want to say how grateful and blessed I was to have so many who offered to help. Only two people told me they could not contribute, and three were not able to complete assignments. That is a remarkable testament to the dedication of a group of leaders who want to see that people get as many opportunities as possible to improve their leadership performance and grow their leadership abilities.

ABOUT THE AUTHOR

Keith Kirkpatrick has had an extraordinary career filled with rich and diverse experiences. Keith is a leader, entrepreneur, innovator, and teacher. He has served at the helm of many organizations and businesses as their CEO, President, Executive Director, or Chair. He has been known as founder, start-up guy, and transformer for over 30 companies and operations. Keith has dedicated his service to a large number of boards and community projects.

Earning recognition as a significant authority on leadership, Keith has been a trusted coach and insightful advisor to many businesses, organizations, and community leaders. Hundreds of students, leaders, and executives have credited him with enhancing their skills and helping them discover and grow their potential.

Keith is a skilled facilitator and engaging presenter. His PBS television talk show aired for nine years with 300 episodes. With a background in a variety of fields and sectors, he has an expanded perspective and a broad understanding of many issues. Keith is a strategic thinker who has spent time teaching at several universities including some in Eastern Europe.

CPSIA information can be obtained
at www.ICGtesting.com
Printed in the USA
BVHW031239281022
650511BV00004B/17